Algebra 2

Applications • Equations • Graphs

Virginia SOL Test
Preparation and Practice

The Standardized Test Practice Workbook provides
practice exercises for every lesson in a standardized test
format. Included are multiple-choice, quantitative-
comparison, and multi-step problems.

McDougal Littell

A DIVISION OF HOUGHTON MIFFLIN COMPANY

ISBN: 0-618-60120-1

1 2 3 4 5 6 7 8 9—MDO—08 07 06 05

Contents

Notes to the Student

Standards of Learning Correlation Presents the Virginia Standards of Learning for Algebra 2 and lists the items related to each standard that appear in the Pre-Course Diagnostic Test and End-of-Course Test in this book.

Pre-Course Diagnostic Test Covers the material from the upcoming textbook. It provides a baseline assessment of each student's knowledge of course content.

Lesson Standardized Test Provides a standardized test for each lesson of the textbook. Items are multiple choice and multi-step.

Cumulative Practice Includes material from several consecutive chapters and can be used to maintain and strengthen skills from earlier lessons.

Test-Taking Tips for Students Summarizes how to prepare for and take standardized tests.

End-of-Course Test Provides a test that covers all the Virginia Standards of Learning for Algebra 2, presented in a format similar to the Virginia Standards of Learning test.

Virginia Standards of Learning Correlation, Algebra 2

Standards of Learning		Pre-Course Diagnostic Test Item	End-of-Course Test Item	Lesson
Expressions and Operations				
AII.1	The student will identify field properties, axioms of equality and inequality, and properties of order that are valid for the set of real numbers and its subsets, complex numbers and matrices.	1, 2, 3	1, 2	1.1, 1.3, 1.6, 4.1, 4.2, 5.4
AII.2	The student will add, subtract, multiply, divide, and simplify rational expressions, including complex fractions.	4, 5, 6	3, 4	9.4, 9.5
AII.3	The student will			
	a) add, subtract, multiply, divide, and simplify radical expressions containing positive rational numbers and variables and expressions containing rational exponents; and	8, 10	5	7.1, 7.2, 7.6
	b) write radical expressions as expression containing rational exponents and vice versa.	7, 9, 11	6	7.1, 7.2
AII.5	The student will identify and factor completely polynomials representing the difference of squares, perfect square trinomials, the sum and difference of cubes, and general trinomials.	12, 13, 14	7, 8	5.2, 6.4, 6.5, 6.6
AII.17	The student will perform operations on complex numbers and express the results in simplest form. Simplifying results will involve using patterns of the powers of i.	15, 16, 17	9, 10	5.4
Relations and Functions				
AII.8	The student will recognize multiple representations of functions (linear, quadratic, absolute value, step, and exponential functions) and convert between a graph, a table, and symbolic form. A transformational approach to graphing will be employed through the use of graphing calculators.	18, 20, 22	11, 12	2.1, 2.7, 2.8, 5.1, 8.1, 8.2

Standards of Learning	Pre-Course Diagnostic Test Item	End-of-Course Test Item	Lesson
Relations and Functions (cont.)			
AII.9 The student will find the domain, range, zeros and inverse of a function; the value of a function for a given element in its domain; and the composition of multiple functions. Functions will include exponential, logarithmic, and those that have domains and ranges that are limited and/or discontinuous. The graphing calculator will be used as a tool to assist in investigation of functions.	19, 21, 25	13, 14, 15	2.1, 7.4, 7.5
AII.15 The student will recognize the general shape of polynomial, exponential, and logarithmic functions. The graphing calculator will be used as a tool to investigate the shape and behavior of these functions.	23, 24, 26	16, 17	6.2, 8.1, 8.2, 8.4
AII.16 The student will investigate and apply the properties of arithmetic and geometric sequences and series to solve practical problems, including writing the first n terms, finding the nth, and evaluating summation formulas. Notation will include Σ and a_n.	27, 28, 29	18, 19	11.1, 11.2, 11.3, 11.4
AII.19 The student will collect and analyze data to make predictions and solve practical problems. Graphing calculators will be used to investigate scatterplots and to determine the equation for a curve of best fit. Models will include linear, quadratic, exponential, and logarithmic functions.	30, 31, 32	20, 21, 22, 23, 24	2.5, 5.8, 8.7
AII.20 The student will identify, create, and solve practical problems involving inverse variation and a combination of direct and inverse variations.	33, 34, 35	25, 26	2.4, 9.1

Virginia Standards of Learning Correlation, Algebra 2 (cont.)

Standards of Learning	Pre-Course Diagnostic Test Item	End-of-Course Test Item	Lesson
Equations and Inequalities			
AII.4 The student will solve absolute value equations and inequalities graphically and algebraically. Graphing calculators will be used as a primary method of solution and to verify algebraic solutions.	37, 38	27, 28, 33, 34	1.7
AII.6 The student will select, justify, and apply a technique to solve a quadratic equation over the set of complex numbers. Graphing calculators will be used for solving and for confirming algebraic solutions.	39, 40, 41	29, 30, 35	5.1, 5.2, 5.3, 5.5, 5.6, 5.7
AII.7 The student will solve equations containing rational expressions and equations containing radical expression algebraically and graphically. Graphing calculators will be used for solving and for confirming the algebraic solutions.	42, 43, 44	31, 32, 36	7.6, 9.6
Analytical Geometry			
AII.10 The student will investigate and describe through the use of graphs the relationships between the solution of an equation, zero of a function, x-intercept of a graph, and factors of a polynomial expression.	45, 46, 47	37, 38, 41	6.7, 6.8
AII.18 The student will identify conic sections (circle, ellipse, parabola, and hyperbola) from his/her equations. Given the equations in (h, k) form, student will sketch graphs of conic sections, using transformations.	48, 49, 50	39, 40, 42	10.2, 10.3, 10.4, 10.5, 10.6

Virginia Standards of Learning Correlation, Algebra 2 (cont.)

Standards of Learning	Pre-Course Diagnostic Test Item	End-of-Course Test Item	Lesson
Systems of Equations/Inequalities			
AII.11 The student will use matrix multiplication to solve practical problems. Graphing calculators or computer programs with matrix capabilities will be used to find the product.	51, 52	43, 44	4.1, 4.2
AII.12 The student will represent problem situations with a system of linear equations and solve the system, using the inverse matrix method. Graphing calculators or computer programs with matrix capability will be used to perform computations.	53, 54	45, 46	3.6, 4.5
AII.13 The student will solve practical problems, using systems of linear inequalities and linear programming, and describe the results both orally and in writing. A graphing calculator will be used to facilitate solutions to linear programming problems.	55, 56, 60	47, 48	3.3, 3.4
AII.14 The student will solve nonlinear systems of equations, including linear-quadratic and quadratic-quadratic, algebraically and graphically. The graphing calculator will be used as a tool to visualize graphs and predict the number of solutions.	57, 58, 59	49, 50	10.7

Name _____   Date _____

Pre-Course Diagnostic Test Answer Sheet

1. Ⓐ Ⓑ Ⓒ Ⓓ   21. Ⓐ Ⓑ Ⓒ Ⓓ   41. Ⓐ Ⓑ Ⓒ Ⓓ
2. Ⓕ Ⓖ Ⓗ Ⓙ   22. Ⓕ Ⓖ Ⓗ Ⓙ   42. Ⓕ Ⓖ Ⓗ Ⓙ
3. Ⓐ Ⓑ Ⓒ Ⓓ   23. Ⓐ Ⓑ Ⓒ Ⓓ   43. Ⓐ Ⓑ Ⓒ Ⓓ
4. Ⓕ Ⓖ Ⓗ Ⓙ   24. Ⓕ Ⓖ Ⓗ Ⓙ   44. Ⓕ Ⓖ Ⓗ Ⓙ
5. Ⓐ Ⓑ Ⓒ Ⓓ   25. Ⓐ Ⓑ Ⓒ Ⓓ   45. Ⓐ Ⓑ Ⓒ Ⓓ
6. Ⓕ Ⓖ Ⓗ Ⓙ   26. Ⓕ Ⓖ Ⓗ Ⓙ   46. Ⓕ Ⓖ Ⓗ Ⓙ
7. Ⓐ Ⓑ Ⓒ Ⓓ   27. Ⓐ Ⓑ Ⓒ Ⓓ   47. Ⓐ Ⓑ Ⓒ Ⓓ
8. Ⓕ Ⓖ Ⓗ Ⓙ   28. Ⓕ Ⓖ Ⓗ Ⓙ   48. Ⓕ Ⓖ Ⓗ Ⓙ
9. Ⓐ Ⓑ Ⓒ Ⓓ   29. Ⓐ Ⓑ Ⓒ Ⓓ   49. Ⓐ Ⓑ Ⓒ Ⓓ
10. Ⓕ Ⓖ Ⓗ Ⓙ   30. Ⓕ Ⓖ Ⓗ Ⓙ   50. Ⓕ Ⓖ Ⓗ Ⓙ
11. Ⓐ Ⓑ Ⓒ Ⓓ   31. Ⓐ Ⓑ Ⓒ Ⓓ   51. Ⓐ Ⓑ Ⓒ Ⓓ
12. Ⓕ Ⓖ Ⓗ Ⓙ   32. Ⓕ Ⓖ Ⓗ Ⓙ   52. Ⓕ Ⓖ Ⓗ Ⓙ
13. Ⓐ Ⓑ Ⓒ Ⓓ   33. Ⓐ Ⓑ Ⓒ Ⓓ   53. Ⓐ Ⓑ Ⓒ Ⓓ
14. Ⓕ Ⓖ Ⓗ Ⓙ   34. Ⓕ Ⓖ Ⓗ Ⓙ   54. Ⓕ Ⓖ Ⓗ Ⓙ
15. Ⓐ Ⓑ Ⓒ Ⓓ   35. Ⓐ Ⓑ Ⓒ Ⓓ   55. Ⓐ Ⓑ Ⓒ Ⓓ
16. Ⓕ Ⓖ Ⓗ Ⓙ   36. Ⓕ Ⓖ Ⓗ Ⓙ   56. Ⓕ Ⓖ Ⓗ Ⓙ
17. Ⓐ Ⓑ Ⓒ Ⓓ   37. Ⓐ Ⓑ Ⓒ Ⓓ   57. Ⓐ Ⓑ Ⓒ Ⓓ
18. Ⓕ Ⓖ Ⓗ Ⓙ   38. Ⓕ Ⓖ Ⓗ Ⓙ   58. Ⓕ Ⓖ Ⓗ Ⓙ
19. Ⓐ Ⓑ Ⓒ Ⓓ   39. Ⓐ Ⓑ Ⓒ Ⓓ   59. Ⓐ Ⓑ Ⓒ Ⓓ
20. Ⓕ Ⓖ Ⓗ Ⓙ   40. Ⓕ Ⓖ Ⓗ Ⓙ   60. Ⓕ Ⓖ Ⓗ Ⓙ

Algebra 2
Standardized Test Practice Workbook

Pre-Course Diagnostic Test

DIRECTIONS
Read and solve each question. For this test you may assume that the value of the denominator of a rational expression is not zero.

1 Which of these statements is *not* true about the set of integers?

  A The commutative property of addition is satisfied.

  B The associative property of multiplication is satisfied.

  C The set has an identity element under addition.

  D The set is closed under division.

2 Which property is illustrated by the equation

$$\frac{1}{3}(4x + 5) = \frac{4x}{3} + \frac{5}{3} \text{ ?}$$

  F Commutative Property of Addition

  G Distributive Property

  H Commutative Property of Multiplication

  J Symmetric Property of Equality

3 Which property is illustrated by the statement

If $a + 3 = b$ and $b = 2c - 5$ then $a + 3 = 2c - 5$?

  A Reflexive Property

  B Symmetric Property

  C Transitive Property

  D Identity Property

4 Which expression is equivalent to

$$\frac{x^2 - 3x + 2}{5x^2 - 5} \text{ ?}$$

  F $\dfrac{x - 2}{5(x - 1)}$

  G $\dfrac{x - 2}{5(x + 1)}$

  H $\dfrac{x + 2}{5(x - 1)}$

  J $\dfrac{x + 2}{5(x + 1)}$

5 Which expression is equivalent to

$$\frac{xy}{\frac{1}{x} + \frac{1}{y}} \text{ ?}$$

  A $\dfrac{1}{x + y}$

  B $\dfrac{xy}{x + y}$

  C $\dfrac{x^2y^2}{x + y}$

  D $\dfrac{x + y}{x^2y^2}$

6 Which fraction is equal to

$$\frac{x + 2}{3x} - \frac{x + 4}{2x} \text{ ?}$$

  F $\dfrac{^-x + 16}{6x}$

  G $\dfrac{^-x - 8}{6x}$

  H $\dfrac{^-x + 6}{6x}$

  J $\dfrac{^-x - 2}{6x}$

7 Which expression is equivalent to $\sqrt[4]{x^7}$?

A $x^{\frac{4}{7}}$

B $x^{\frac{7}{4}}$

C x^3

D x^{11}

8 What is the value of $\sqrt[3]{\dfrac{1}{27}}$?

F $\dfrac{1}{9}$

G $\dfrac{1}{3}$

H 3

J 9

9 Which of these has the same value as $z^{\frac{9}{5}}$?

A $\sqrt[9]{z^5}$

B $\sqrt[9]{z^4}$

C $\sqrt[5]{z^9}$

D $\sqrt[4]{z^5}$

10 Which has the same value as $\sqrt[3]{w^{12}x^6y^9}$?

F $w^4x^2y^3$

G $w^9x^3y^6$

H $w^{15}x^9y^{12}$

J $w^{36}x^{18}y^{27}$

11 Which is *not* another way to write the expression $\sqrt[4]{n^2}$?

A $n^{0.5}$

B n^2

C $n^{\frac{1}{2}}$

D $\sqrt{n}$

12 Which is the complete factorization of $16x^2 - 4y^2$?

F $(4x + 2y)^2$

G $4(12x^2 - y^2)$

H $(4x - 2y)(x + 2y)$

J $4(2x - y)(2x + y)$

13 Which is the complete factorization of $x^3 - 8$?

A $(x - 2)(x^2 + 2x - 4)$

B $(x + 2)(x^2 - 2x + 4)$

C $(x - 2)(x^2 + 2x + 4)$

D $(x - 2)(x^2 - 2x + 4)$

14 Which expression shows the complete factorization of $mr + nr - ms - ns$?

F $(m + r)(n - s)$

G $(m + s)(n - r)$

H $(m + n)(r - s)$

J $(m + n)(r + s)$

15 What is the value of i^{14}?

   A i

   B $^-1$

   C ^-i

   D 1

16 What is the product of $(5 + 4i)$ and $(3 - 2i)$?

   F $7 + 2i$

   G $8 + 2i$

   H $15 - 8i$

   J $23 + 2i$

17 Which of the following complex numbers is equal to $\frac{3 - 2i}{2 - i}$?

   A $\frac{8 + i}{5}$

   B $\frac{8 - i}{5}$

   C $\frac{^-8 + i}{5}$

   D $\frac{^-8 - i}{5}$

18

X	0	1	2	3	4	5
f(x)	1	2	4	8	16	32

What type of function is represented by the values in the table?

   F Exponential

   G Linear

   H Quadratic

   J Step

19 If $f(x) = \frac{1}{x}$, what is $f^{-1}(x)$?

   A $f-1(x) = -\frac{1}{x}$

   B $f^{-1}(x) = \frac{1}{x}$

   C $f^{-1}(x) = x$

   D $f^{-1}(x) = {}^-x$

20

X	$^-5$	$^-1$	0	1	5
f(x)	$^-7$	1	3	5	13

Which function is represented by this table?

   F $y = x + 2$

   G $y = 2x + 3$

   H $y = 2x - 3$

   J $y = x^2 + 3$

21 If $f(x) = 2^x$ what is $f(-3)$?

   A -8

   B $-\frac{1}{8}$

   C $\frac{1}{8}$

   D 8

22

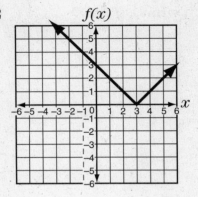

Which function is shown in the graph?

F $f(x) = |x| + 3$

G $f(x) = |x| - 3$

H $f(x) = |x + 3|$

J $f(x) = |x - 3|$

23

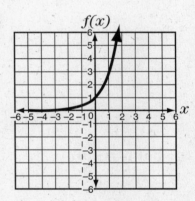

What type of function is shown in the graph above?

A Exponential

B Logarithmic

C Quadratic

D Cubic

24 Which statement is true about the graph of $y = \ln x$?

F The graph has a horizontal asymptote at $y = e$.

G The graph crosses the x-axis at exactly one point.

H The domain of the graph is the set of all real numbers.

J The y-intercept of the graph is 1.

25 What is the range of $f(x) = (x - 2)^2$?

A all real numbers

B all real numbers greater than or equal to 0

C all real numbers greater than or equal to 2

D all real numbers less than or equal to 0

26 What could be the degree of the polynomial graphed below?

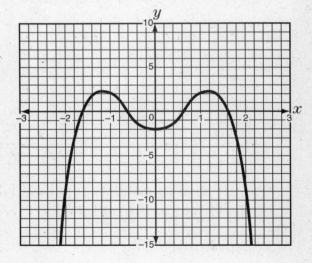

F 2

G 3

H 4

J 5

27 What is the sum of the series

$$\sum_{n=1}^{4} (3n + 2)\ ?$$

   A 14

   B 32

   C 38

   D 48

28 What are the first four terms of the sequence $a_n = 2^{n-1}$?

   F $\{0, 1, 3, 7\}$

   G $\{1, 2, 4, 8\}$

   H $\left\{\frac{1}{2}, 1, 2, 4\right\}$

   J $\left\{1, \frac{1}{2}, \frac{1}{4}, \frac{1}{8}\right\}$

29 If $a_n = \frac{1}{4}n + 3$, what is the value of a_8?

   A 2

   B 5

   C 11

   D 13

30 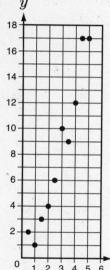 Which of these could be an equation for a line of best fit for the data in the scatterplot?

   F $y = 3x - 1$

   G $y = 3x + 1$

   H $y = 4x - 1$

   J $y = 4x + 1$

31 Which type of function would best fit the data in this scatterplot?

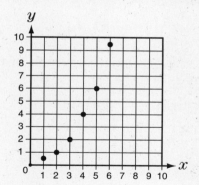

   A Linear

   B Quadratic

   C Logarithmic

   D Exponential

32 Which of these could be the equation for a curve of best fit for the data?

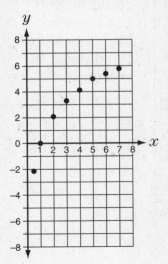

F $y = 3 \ln x$

G $y = \ln 3x$

H $y = 3 + \ln x$

J $y = 3 + \ln 3x$

33 If x and y vary directly, which of the following is true?

A the product xy is constant

B the sum $x + y$ is constant

C the ratio $\frac{y}{x}$ is constant

D the difference $y - x$ is constant

34 The number of revolutions per minute a gear makes varies inversely as the number of teeth on the gear. One gear has 36 teeth and makes 30 revolutions per minute. Another gear has 24 teeth. How many revolutions per minute will this gear make?

F 20

G 29

H 45

J 60

35 The velocity v of sound in air varies directly as the square root of the absolute temperature t of the air. Which equation shows this relationship?

A $v = k\sqrt{t}$

B $v\sqrt{t} = k$

C $t = kv^2$

D $vt^2 = k$

36 Which graph shows the solution set for $|8x - 4| \le 28$?

F

G

H

J

37 What are the solutions of $|5 - 6x| = 13$?

A $^-3$ and $^-1\frac{1}{3}$

B $^-3$ and $1\frac{1}{3}$

C $^-1\frac{1}{3}$ and 3

D $1\frac{1}{3}$ and 3

38 What are all of the solutions of $|6x + 18| \ge 12$?

F $x \ge ^-1$ or $x \le ^-5$

G $x \ge 1$ or $x \le 5$

H $x \le ^-1$ or $x \ge ^-5$

J $x \le 1$ or $x \ge 5$

39 Which constant can be added to both sides of the quadratic equation $x^2 + 4x = 2$ to solve it by completing the square?

   A 2

   B 4

   C 8

   D 16

40 If $a > 0$, for what values of c are the solutions of $ax^2 + c = 0$ imaginary?

   F $c < 0$

   G $c > 0$

   H $c \leq 0$

   J $c \geq 0$

41 For what values of c are the roots of $3x^2 - 2x + c = 0$ real numbers?

   A $c < \frac{1}{3}$

   B $c \leq \frac{1}{3}$

   C $c > \frac{1}{3}$

   D $c \geq \frac{1}{3}$

42 What is the solution to the equation

$$\sqrt{x - 3} + 5 = 12 ?$$

   F $x = 7$

   G $x = 10$

   H $x = 46$

   J $x = 52$

43 What are the solutions of

$$\frac{30}{x} - \frac{18}{2x} = 7x ?$$

   A $x = \pm \frac{1}{3}$

   B $x = \pm 3$

   C $x = \pm \frac{1}{\sqrt{3}}$

   D $x = \pm \sqrt{3}$

44 The graphs of the functions $y = \frac{3}{x + 2}$ and $y = \frac{3x}{2x + 1}$ are shown below.

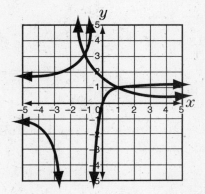

For what values of x is $\frac{3}{x + 2} = \frac{3x}{2x + 1}$?

   F $x = {}^-1$ and $x = 3$

   G $x = {}^-1$ and $x = 1$

   H $x = 0$ and $x = 1$

   J $x = 1$ and $x = 3$

45 The graph of a cubic function is shown below.

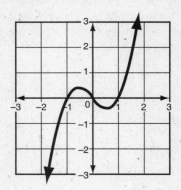

Which is an equation of this function?

A $y = x(x + 1)^2$

B $y = x(x - 1)^2$

C $y = (x + 1)(x - 1)$

D $y = x(x + 1)(x - 1)$

46 What are the zeros of the function graphed below?

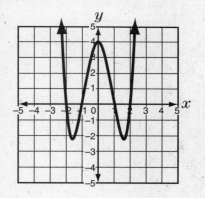

F $^-1$ and 1

G $^-2$ and 2

H $^-2, ^-1, 1,$ and 2

J $^-2, 0, 2,$ and 4

47 The graph of a quadratic function is shown below.

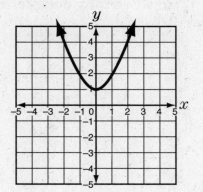

Which of these best describes the zero(s) of the function?

A 1 real zero

B 1 imaginary zero

C 2 real zeros

D 2 imaginary zeros

48 What are the coordinates of the center of the conic section whose equation is $\dfrac{(x - 1)^2}{9} + \dfrac{(y + 2)^2}{4} = 1$?

F $(^-1, ^-2)$

G $(^-1, 2)$

H $(1, ^-2)$

J $(1, 2)$

49 The equation $\dfrac{y^2}{9} - \dfrac{x^2}{4} = 1$ represents what kind of conic section?

A Circle

B Ellipse

C Hyperbola

D Parabola

50 Which of these shows the graph of a conic section with an equation of $\frac{(x-3)^2}{4} + \frac{(y-2)^2}{16} = 1$?

F

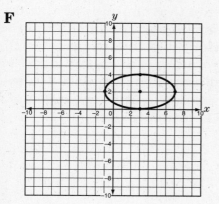

G

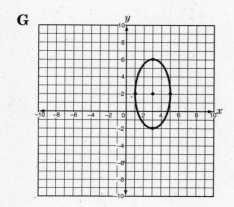

H

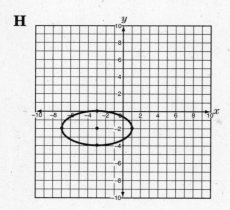

J

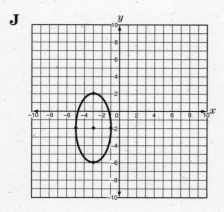

51 Three clothing stores each sell 3 brands of running shoes. The matrices below show the number of pairs sold at each store, and the cost of each pair of shoes.

Pairs Sold

	Brand 1	Brand 2	Brand 3
Store A	15	22	18
Store B	7	8	5
Store C	12	14	10

Cost

	Dollars
Brand 1	25.99
Brand 2	29.99
Brand 3	35.99

Which matrix shows the total sales for each store?

A

	Cost Dollars
Store A	1697.45
Store B	601.80
Store C	1091.64

B

	Cost Dollars
Store A	1669.45
Store B	597.80
Store C	1083.64

C

	Cost Dollars
Store A	1667.45
Store B	621.80
Store C	1111.64

D

	Cost Dollars
Store A	1651.45
Store B	609.80
Store C	1095.64

52 The school cafeteria currently sells three types of drinks as shown in the table below.

	Small	Large
Milk	$0.30	$0.80
Tomato Juice	$0.60	$0.90
Orange Juice	$0.80	$1.20

The manager of the cafeteria plans on raising these prices by 50%. Which matrix shows the new prices of the drinks?

F

	Small	Large
Milk	$0.15	$0.40
Tomato Juice	$0.30	$0.45
Orange Juice	$0.40	$0.60

G

	Small	Large
Milk	$0.45	$0.95
Tomato Juice	$0.75	$1.05
Orange Juice	$0.95	$1.35

H

	Small	Large
Milk	$0.80	$1.30
Tomato Juice	$1.10	$1.40
Orange Juice	$1.30	$1.70

J

	Small	Large
Milk	$0.45	$1.20
Tomato Juice	$0.90	$1.35
Orange Juice	$1.20	$1.80

53 A chemist has two beakers with solutions of water and acid. She has x mL of a solution that contains 15% acid by volume, and y mL of a solution that contains 35% acid by volume. She wants to mix the two solutions together to produce 10 mL of a solution that contains 20% acid by volume. Which matrix equation can she use to find how much of each solution to use?

A $\begin{bmatrix} 1 & 1 \\ 0.15 & 0.35 \end{bmatrix} \begin{bmatrix} x \\ y \end{bmatrix} = \begin{bmatrix} 10 \\ 2 \end{bmatrix}$

B $\begin{bmatrix} 1 & 0.15 \\ 1 & 0.35 \end{bmatrix} \begin{bmatrix} x \\ y \end{bmatrix} = \begin{bmatrix} 10 \\ 2 \end{bmatrix}$

C $\begin{bmatrix} 1 & 1 \\ 0.15 & 0.35 \end{bmatrix} \begin{bmatrix} x & y \end{bmatrix} = \begin{bmatrix} 10 & 2 \end{bmatrix}$

D $\begin{bmatrix} 1 & 1 \\ 0.15 & 0.35 \end{bmatrix} \begin{bmatrix} x & y \end{bmatrix} = \begin{bmatrix} 10 \\ 2 \end{bmatrix}$

54 What is the solution of the matrix equation below

$$\begin{bmatrix} 3 & 3 & ^-1 \\ ^-5 & ^-4 & 2 \\ ^-2 & ^-2 & 1 \end{bmatrix} x = \begin{bmatrix} 3 \\ ^-7 \\ ^-3 \end{bmatrix}$$

A $\begin{bmatrix} ^-3 \\ ^-1 \\ 1 \end{bmatrix}$

B $\begin{bmatrix} ^-1 \\ 1 \\ 3 \end{bmatrix}$

C $\begin{bmatrix} 1 \\ ^-1 \\ ^-3 \end{bmatrix}$

D $\begin{bmatrix} 3 \\ 1 \\ ^-1 \end{bmatrix}$

55 The graph of the system of constraints in a linear programming problem appears below.

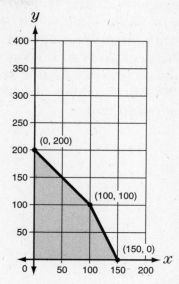

If the objective function for the problem is $P = 8x + 5y$, what are the values of x and y that maximize P?

A (0, 200)

B (50, 150)

C (100, 100)

D (150, 0)

56 The members of a community association are going to make and sell fruit baskets. They will make two sizes: small and large. They will earn $3 for each small and $4 for each large fruit basket they sell. The organizer of the sale constructed this feasible region to show the possible numbers of fruit baskets they could make.

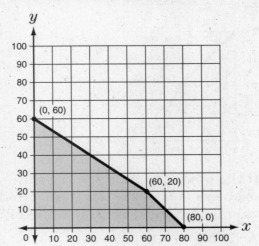

If x represents the number of small baskets and y represents the number of large baskets, how many of each size should they make to earn the most profit?

F 0 small baskets and 60 large baskets

G 20 small baskets and 60 large baskets

H 60 small baskets and 20 large baskets

J 80 small baskets and 0 large baskets

57 What is the solution set for the system of equations below?

$$\begin{cases} y = x^2 + 5x \\ y = 2x + 4 \end{cases}$$

A $\{(^-4, \,^-36), (1, 6)\}$

B $\{(^-4, \,^-4), (1, 6)\}$

C $\{(^-1, \,^-4), (4, 36)\}$

D $\{(^-1, 2), (4, 12)\}$

58 How many solutions does this system of equations have?

$$\begin{cases} y = x^2 - 4x \\ y = ^-2x^2 + 2x - 5 \end{cases}$$

F 0

G 1

H 2

J 4

59 What is the greatest number of points of intersection between the graph of a quadratic function and the graph of a cubic function?

A 1

B 2

C 3

D 4

60 Which of the following points lies in the solution set of $y \le \frac{1}{2}x - 3$ and $y \le ^-4x - 4$?

F $(^-6, 3)$

G $(^-2, \,^-7)$

H $(2, \,^-1)$

J $(4, \,^-5)$

NAME _____ DATE _____

Standardized Test Practice

For use with pages 3–10

TEST TAKING STRATEGY   Spend no more than a few minutes on each question.

1. *Multiple Choice*   Which list of numbers is written in increasing order?

   Ⓐ $-3.4, -\frac{11}{3}, 0, 2.3, 5$

   Ⓑ $-7, -6.3, -\sqrt{37}, 2, 2.2$

   Ⓒ $-1.2, -\sqrt{3}, -1, -\frac{1}{3}, -0.6$

   Ⓓ $-\sqrt{7}, -2.5, 1.8, \sqrt{3}, \sqrt{2}$

   Ⓔ $-\frac{3}{5}, -0.4, 0.3, \frac{1}{4}, 1$

2. *Multiple Choice*   Which property is illustrated by the statement $3(7 + 5) = 3(7) + 3(5)$?

   Ⓐ Associative property of addition

   Ⓑ Commutative property of addition

   Ⓒ Commutative property of multiplication

   Ⓓ Associative property of multiplication

   Ⓔ Distributive property

3. *Multiple Choice*   Which number does $(-16) - (-14)$ equal?

   Ⓐ -30 Ⓑ 30 Ⓒ 2

   Ⓓ -2 Ⓔ 224

4. *Multiple Choice*   Which number does $63 \div (-9)$ equal?

   Ⓐ $-\frac{1}{8}$ Ⓑ -7 Ⓒ 7

   Ⓓ $-\frac{1}{7}$ Ⓔ -8

Quantitative Comparison   **In Exercises 5–9, choose the statement below that is true about the given quantities.**

   Ⓐ The number in column A is greater.

   Ⓑ The number in column B is greater.

   Ⓒ The two numbers are equal.

   Ⓓ The relationship cannot be determined from the given information.

	Column A	Column B
5.	-4.4	$-\sqrt{20}$
6.	$(-3) + (-15)$	$(-9)(2)$
7.	$29 + (-34)$	$34 - 29$
8.	$(-28) \div (7)$	$52 \div 13$
9.	$(-10) - (-13)$	$13 - 10$

10. *Multiple Choice*   At 7:00 A.M. the temperature was 13°F. By 5:00 P.M. the temperature had dropped to -4°F. Which number represents the degree change in temperature during this period of time?

   Ⓐ 9 Ⓑ 17 Ⓒ 11

   Ⓓ -9 Ⓔ -17

Algebra 2
Standardized Test Practice Workbook

Standardized Test Practice

For use with pages 11–18

TEST TAKING STRATEGY Draw an arrow on your test booklet next to questions that you do not answer. This will enable you to find the questions quickly when you go back.

1. *Multiple Choice* Which expression using exponents corresponds to "x to the fourth power?"

   (A) 4^x (B) $x \cdot x \cdot x \cdot x$

   (C) $x^{\frac{1}{4}}$ (D) x^4

   (E) $4x$

2. *Multiple Choice* Which number does $28 \div 4 + 1 \cdot 6$ equal?

   (A) 48   (B) 13

   (C) $\dfrac{14}{5}$ (D) $\dfrac{5}{14}$

   (E) 43

3. *Multiple Choice* Which number does $16 - 8 \div 4 \cdot 3$ equal?

   (A) 10   (B) 6

   (C) $\dfrac{2}{3}$ (D) 42

   (E) 22

4. *Multiple Choice* Which number does $5x - 3$ equal when $x = 2$?

   (A) 1   (B) -7

   (C) 4   (D) -1

   (E) 7

Quantitative Comparison **In Exercises 5–8, choose the statement below that is true about the given quantities.**

   (A) The number in column A is greater.

   (B) The number in column B is greater.

   (C) The two numbers are equal.

   (D) The relationship cannot be determined from the given information.

	Column A	Column B
5.	$2 + 6 \div 3$	4
6.	$15 \div (3 + 2)$	$15 \div 3 + 2$
7.	6	$(4 - 8) \cdot 3$
8.	$4x$	$7 - 5 \cdot 2$

9. *Multiple Choice* Which number does $(x + 1)^2 + 3x$ equal when $x = -2$?

   (A) -4 (B) 3

   (C) 12   (D) 7

   (E) -5

10. *Multiple Choice* Which number does $x^2 - 2x + 1$ equal when $x = -1$?

   (A) 2   (B) 0

   (C) 4   (D) -1

   (E) -2

NAME _____ DATE _____

Standardized Test Practice

For use with pages 19–25

TEST TAKING STRATEGY   **Read the test questions carefully. Also try to find short cuts that will help you move through the questions quicker.**

1. *Multiple Choice*   Which number is the solution of the equation $2x + 3 = -7$?

  Ⓐ -2 Ⓑ -5

  Ⓒ 2 Ⓓ 5

  Ⓔ $\dfrac{1}{2}$

2. *Multiple Choice*   Which number is the solution of the equation $5x + 6 = -3x - 2$?

  Ⓐ 2 Ⓑ -2

  Ⓒ 4 Ⓓ -1

  Ⓔ 1

3. *Multiple Choice*   Which number is the solution of the equation $-\frac{1}{2}x + 3 = 2(2x - 3)$?

  Ⓐ -4 Ⓑ 2

  Ⓒ $\dfrac{1}{2}$ Ⓓ -2

  Ⓔ 4

4. *Multiple Choice*   A sales clerk's base salary is $21,000. The clerk earns a 6% commission on total sales. How much must the clerk sell to earn $30,000 total?

  Ⓐ $15,000   Ⓑ $1,500

  Ⓒ $150   Ⓓ $15

  Ⓔ $150,000

5. *Multi-Step Problem*   You are in charge of planting a rectangular garden with a length of 10 meters and a width of 8 meters. There is to be a stone border of uniform width surrounding the entire garden.

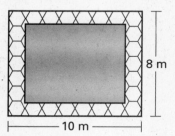

  8 m

  —— 10 m ——

a. What is the total area of the rectangular garden including the stone border?

b. What is the area of the stone border if the total area of the planted garden is 63 square meters?

c. If stone costs $4.25 per square meter, how much will installing the stone border cost?

d. *Critical Thinking*   If you have an allowance of $100 to spend on the stone border, explain whether it is possible to increase the size of the border by 0.25 meter on all sides. (*Hint:* Assume increasing the size of the border reduces the length and width of the planted garden.)

6. *Multiple Choice*   Which number is the solution of the equation $-2x + 3 = 3x - 7$?

  Ⓐ -2 Ⓑ 2 Ⓒ 4

  Ⓓ -4 Ⓔ $\dfrac{1}{4}$

7. *Multiple Choice*   Which number is the solution of the equation $5(2x + 6) = -3(3x + 2) + x$?

  Ⓐ -2 Ⓑ 2 Ⓒ $\dfrac{4}{3}$

  Ⓓ 12 Ⓔ -12

NAME _____   DATE _____

Standardized Test Practice

For use with pages 26–32

TEST TAKING STRATEGY **If you find yourself spending too much time on one test question and getting frustrated, move on to the next question. You can revisit a difficult problem later with a fresh perspective.**

1. *Multiple Choice* Given the equation $y = 2x - 5$, find the value of y when $x = 3$.

Ⓐ 18   Ⓑ −1   Ⓒ 11

Ⓓ 0   Ⓔ 1

2. *Multiple Choice* Solve $5x - 2y = -3$ for y.

Ⓐ $y = -5x - 3$ Ⓑ $y = -\frac{5}{2}x - 3$

Ⓒ $y = \frac{5}{2}x + \frac{3}{2}$ Ⓓ $y = \frac{5}{2}x - \frac{3}{2}$

Ⓔ $y = -\frac{5}{2}x + \frac{3}{2}$

3. *Multiple Choice* Which gives the equation $P = 2l + 2w$ solved for l?

Ⓐ $l = P - w$ Ⓑ $l = \frac{P - 2w}{2}$

Ⓒ $l = P - \frac{w}{2}$ Ⓓ $l = -\frac{w}{2}$

Ⓔ $l = \frac{w}{2}$

4. *Multiple Choice* You have 24 feet of fencing with which to enclose a rectangular garden. Express the garden's area in terms of its width.

Ⓐ $A = w(24 - w)$ Ⓑ $A = w(24 - 2w)$
Ⓒ $A = w(12 - w)$ Ⓓ $A = w(12 - 2w)$
Ⓔ $A = 2w(12 - w)$

Quantitative Comparison **In Exercises 5–8, choose the statement below that is true about the given quantities if $2x + 3y = 10$.**

Ⓐ The number in column A is greater.

Ⓑ The number in column B is greater.

Ⓒ The two numbers are equal.

Ⓓ The relationship cannot be determined from the given information.

	Column A	Column B
5.	$x = -1$	y
6.	$x = 5$	y
7.	x	$y = 4$
8.	x	y

9. *Multiple Choice* Solve $-x - 3y = 7$ for y.

Ⓐ $y = x + \frac{7}{3}$ Ⓑ $y = \frac{x}{3} + \frac{7}{3}$

Ⓒ $y = -\frac{x}{3} + \frac{7}{3}$ Ⓓ $y = -\frac{x}{3} - \frac{7}{3}$

Ⓔ $y = -\frac{x}{3} + 7$

10. *Multiple Choice* Which gives the equation $I = Prt$ solved for r?

Ⓐ $r = \frac{Pt}{I}$ Ⓑ $r = \frac{I}{Pt}$

Ⓒ $r = \frac{P}{I} - t$ Ⓓ $r = I - Pt$

Ⓔ $r = I - \frac{P}{t}$

NAME _____ DATE _____

Standardized Test Practice

For use with pages 33–40

TEST TAKING STRATEGY   **Do not panic if you run out of time before answering all of the questions. You can still receive a high score on a standardized test without answering every question.**

1. *Multiple Choice*   You have borrowed $284 from your parents to pay for a school ski trip. Your parents are not charging you interest, but they want to be repaid as soon as possible. If you can afford to repay them $24 a week, how long will it take for you to repay the loan?

   (A) 11 weeks   (B) 12 weeks

   (C) 13 weeks   (D) 10 weeks

   (E) 14 weeks

2. *Multiple Choice*   A rectangular box measures 25 centimeters long, 17 centimeters high, and 15 centimeters wide. How much wrapping paper is required in order to wrap the box?

   (A) 6375 cm³   (B) 57 cm

   (C) 2110 cm²   (D) 1055 cm²

   (E) 6375 cm²

3. *Multiple Choice*   If you drive 364 miles and you average 18.2 miles per gallon, how much do you spend on gasoline if it costs $1.32 per gallon?

   (A) $26.40   (B) $26.00

   (C) $25.40   (D) $26.25

   (E) $25.00

4. *Multiple Choice*   You are buying new carpet for your bedroom which measures 12 feet long by 14 feet wide. How much will the new carpet cost if it sells for $4.75 per square foot?

   (A) $123.50   (B) $79.80

   (C) $1,235.00   (D) $247.00

   (E) $798.00

5. *Multi-Step Problem*   You have a part-time job in which your employer pays you $6.25 an hour for working 6 hours per week. You are paid $7.25 an hour for each additional hour over 6 hours.

   a. Write a verbal model that would give you the total amount of pay for working part-time.

   b. Assign labels to your verbal model from part (a).

   c. Write an algebraic model from part (b).

   d. Solve the algebraic model if you work 9 hours per week.

   e. *Critical Thinking*   If your employer offers to pay you $.50 more per hour for each additional hour over 10 hours, what will your pay be if you work 12 hours per week?

6. *Multiple Choice*   You are taking guitar lessons. The cost of the first lesson is twice the cost of each additional lesson. You spend $360 for 8 lessons. How much did the first lesson cost?

   (A) $40   (B) $45

   (C) $50   (D) $60

   (E) $80

7. *Multiple Choice*   You are selling candy bars that cost $1.25 each. Your family bought 15 bars. How many more bars must you sell in order to collect $115?

   (A) 40 bars   (B) 52 bars

   (C) 74 bars   (D) 77 bars

   (E) 80 bars

Standardized Test Practice

For use with pages 41–48

TEST TAKING STRATEGY During the test, do not worry excessively about how much time you have left. Concentrate on the question in front of you.

1. *Multiple Choice* Which inequality is the solution of $-5x < 15$?

   (A) $x < -3$ (B) $x < -\dfrac{1}{3}$

   (C) $x > -\dfrac{1}{3}$ (D) $x > 3$

   (E) $x > -3$

2. *Multiple Choice* Which inequality is the solution of $2x - 1 \le 4x + 3$?

   (A) $x < -2$ (B) $x \ge -2$

   (C) $x \le -2$ (D) $x \ge 2$

   (E) $x > -2$

3. *Multiple Choice* Which inequality is the solution of $3(x - 2) \ge x + 10$?

   (A) $x \le 8$ (B) $x \ge 6$

   (C) $x \ge -8$ (D) $x \ge 8$

   (E) $x \le 6$

4. *Multiple Choice* Which number is *not* a solution of the inequality $-3 < 2x + 5 < 7$?

   (A) 0 (B) -2

   (C) $-\dfrac{3}{4}$ (D) $\dfrac{1}{3}$

   (E) -4

5. *Multi-Step Problem* Your English teacher announces that course grades will be computed by taking 45% of your research paper score (0–100 points) and adding 55% of your final exam score (0–100 points).

   a. If you score 84 points on the research paper, how many points will be considered in computing your course grade?

   b. If you score 92 points on the final exam, how many points will be considered in computing your course grade?

   c. What will your course grade be, based on the scores given in parts (a) and (b)? (Assume that scores will be rounded up.)

   d. Since you scored 84 points on the research paper, what scores can you get on the final exam to get a course grade of at least 90?

   e. *Critical Thinking* If you had scored 10 points more (94 points) on the research paper, could you score 5 fewer points on the final exam (87 points) and still get a course grade of at least 90?

6. *Multiple Choice* Which number is *not* a solution of the inequality $6 \le x + 12 \le 15$?

   (A) -4 (B) 3

   (C) -8 (D) 1

   (E) 0

7. *Multiple Choice* Which number is *not* a solution of the compound inequality $3x - 2 < 7$ or $-2x - 3 < -15$?

   (A) 8 (B) 4

   (C) -5 (D) 7

   (E) 0

Algebra 2
Standardized Test Practice Workbook

Chapter 1

NAME _____ DATE _____

Standardized Test Practice

For use with pages 51–55

TEST TAKING STRATEGY **When taking a test, first tackle the questions that you know are easy for you to answer.**

1. *Multiple Choice* Which number is a solution of the equation $|2x - 1| = 5$?

   Ⓐ 2   Ⓑ -3

   Ⓒ $-\dfrac{5}{2}$ Ⓓ -2

   Ⓔ $\dfrac{5}{2}$

2. *Multiple Choice* Which number is a solution of the equation $|5x + 2| = 12$?

   Ⓐ -2 Ⓑ $-\dfrac{14}{5}$

   Ⓒ $\dfrac{14}{5}$ Ⓓ $-\dfrac{2}{5}$

   Ⓔ $\dfrac{2}{5}$

3. *Multiple Choice* Which number is *not* a solution of the inequality $|3x + 4| \le 6$?

   Ⓐ 0   Ⓑ $\dfrac{2}{3}$

   Ⓒ -3 Ⓓ -1

   Ⓔ 1

4. *Multiple Choice* Which number is *not* a solution of the inequality $|2x - 5| > 9$?

   Ⓐ 8   Ⓑ -3

   Ⓒ -5 Ⓓ -4

   Ⓔ 3

Quantitative Comparison **In Exercises 5–9, choose the statement below that is true about the given quantities.**

   Ⓐ The number in column A is greater.

   Ⓑ The number in column B is greater.

   Ⓒ The two numbers are equal.

   Ⓓ The relationship cannot be determined from the given information.

	Column A	Column B
5.	$\|2x - 3\| = 5$	-5
6.	11	$\|x + 3\| = 8$
7.	$\|x - 3\| = 4$	$\|3 - x\| = 4$
8.	$\frac{1}{2}$	$\|4x + 5\| = 3$
9.	$\|6x + 1\| \le 13$	3

10. *Multiple Choice* Which graph represents $|x + 2| > 5$?

    Ⓐ

    Ⓑ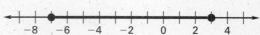

    Ⓒ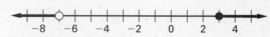

    Ⓓ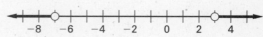

    Ⓔ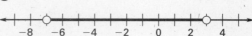

Chapter 1

NAME _____ DATE _____

Standardized Test Practice

For use with pages 67–74

TEST TAKING STRATEGY   **During a test it is important to stay mentally focused, but also physically relaxed.**

1. *Multiple Choice*   Which of the following relations is *not* a function?

Ⓐ
x	2	3	4
y	1	1	1

Ⓑ
x	0	2	2
y	4	1	3

Ⓒ
x	7	5	3
y	7	5	3

Ⓓ
x	6	5	4
y	1	2	3

Ⓔ
x	1	2	4
y	4	0	3

2. *Multiple Choice*   Which of the following relations is *not* a function?

Ⓐ
x	2	4	6
y	1	3	5

Ⓑ
x	0	1	2
y	0	1	2

Ⓒ
x	4	6	8
y	8	6	4

Ⓓ
x	5	6	7
y	2	3	3

Ⓔ
x	3	3	6
y	1	4	7

3. *Multiple Choice*   If $g(x) = x^2 + 3x - 5$, what is $g(-2)$?

Ⓐ -7 Ⓑ 5

Ⓒ -1 Ⓓ -3

Ⓔ -15

4. *Multiple Choice*   Which of the following is a linear function?

Ⓐ $g(x) = 2x^2 - x + 1$

Ⓑ $h(x) = |x + 1|$

Ⓒ $f(x) = 2x - 5$

Ⓓ $g(x) = -x^3 - 1$

Ⓔ $h(x) = \sqrt{x - 4}$

Quantitative Comparison   **In Exercises 5–9, choose the statement below that is true about the given quantities.**

Ⓐ   The number in column A is greater.

Ⓑ   The number in column B is greater.

Ⓒ   The two numbers are equal.

Ⓓ   The relationship cannot be determined from the given information.

	Column A	Column B
5.	$f(x) = x^2 - 3$ when $x = 1$	$f(x) = 2x^2 + 1$ when $x = 0$
6.	$f(x) = x^2 + 3x$ when $x = -1$	$f(x) = 3x^2 - 4$ when $x = 1$
7.	$f(x) = x^2 + 5x - 6$	$f(x) = 2x^2 - 3x - 1$
8.	$f(x) = x^2 - x - 1$ when $x = 2$	$f(x) = x^2 + 2x - 2$ when $x = 1$
9.	$f(x) = 5x^2 - 2x + 1$ when $x = -2$	$f(x) = x^2$ when $x = -5$

Algebra 2
Standardized Test Practice Workbook

NAME _____ DATE _____

Standardized Test Practice

For use with pages 75–81

TEST TAKING STRATEGY   **Read the test questions carefully.**

1. *Multiple Choice*   What is the slope of the line that passes through $(-5, 4)$ and $(-1, 8)$?

   Ⓐ $-\dfrac{2}{3}$ Ⓑ -1

   Ⓒ $\dfrac{3}{2}$ Ⓓ 1

   Ⓔ $\dfrac{2}{3}$

2. *Multiple Choice*   What is the slope of the line that passes through $(2, 5)$ and $(-4, 3)$?

   Ⓐ $\dfrac{1}{3}$ Ⓑ 3

   Ⓒ -3 Ⓓ $-\dfrac{1}{3}$

   Ⓔ 1

3. *Multiple Choice*   Which of the following lines is the steepest?

   Ⓐ Line 1: through $(4, 5)$ and $(3, 2)$

   Ⓑ Line 2: through $(6, 4)$ and $(3, 2)$

   Ⓒ Line 3: through $(-2, 7)$ and $(6, 6)$

   Ⓓ Line 4: through $(-1, 3)$ and $(4, 5)$

   Ⓔ Line 5: through $(-2, -4)$ and $(1, 2)$

4. *Multiple Choice*   The line that passes through the points $(3, 0)$ and $(-5, 8)$ ___?___.

   Ⓐ is vertical   Ⓑ falls

   Ⓒ is horizontal   Ⓓ rises

   Ⓔ doesn't exist

5. *Multi-Step Problem*   You are in charge of building the roof for a warehouse. It is a requirement that the pitch or slope of the roof rises at least 3 feet for every 15 feet of horizontal distance.

   a. What is the required pitch or slope of the roof?

   b. If the warehouse is 120 feet wide, what is the minimum required height of the roof?

   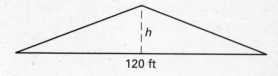

   120 ft

   c. Use the Pythagorean theorem to determine the length of one side of the roof.

   d. *Writing*   Explain how a roof height of 15 feet meets the required pitch for the roof.

6. *Multiple Choice*   A ladder 40 feet in length that hits the wall at a height of 24 feet has a slope of ___?___.

   Ⓐ $\dfrac{3}{4}$ Ⓑ $\dfrac{4}{3}$

   Ⓒ $\dfrac{3}{5}$ Ⓓ $\dfrac{5}{3}$

   Ⓔ $\dfrac{4}{5}$

7. *Multiple Choice*   If a line passes through $(3, 8)$ and $(3, -4)$ then the line ___?___.

   Ⓐ rises   Ⓑ falls

   Ⓒ is horizontal   Ⓓ is vertical

   Ⓔ doesn't exist

NAME _____ DATE _____

Standardized Test Practice

For use with pages 82–88

TEST TAKING STRATEGY   **If you find yourself spending too much time on one question and getting frustrated, move on to the next question.**

1. *Multiple Choice*   What is the slope of the line $y = -\frac{1}{5}x - 7$?

   Ⓐ $\frac{1}{5}$ Ⓑ -7

   Ⓒ -5 Ⓓ $-\frac{1}{5}$

   Ⓔ 7

2. *Multiple Choice*   What is the *y*-intercept of the line $y = \frac{2}{3}x + \frac{4}{5}$?

   Ⓐ $\frac{2}{3}$ Ⓑ $\frac{4}{5}$

   Ⓒ $-\frac{4}{5}$ Ⓓ $-\frac{2}{3}$

   Ⓔ $\frac{5}{4}$

3. *Multiple Choice*   What is the *x*-intercept of the line $y = -\frac{1}{4}x - 16$?

   Ⓐ $-\frac{1}{4}$ Ⓑ -16

   Ⓒ 64 Ⓓ 4

   Ⓔ -64

4. *Multiple Choice*   What is the *y*-intercept and the *x*-intercept of the line $y = -5x - 15$?

   Ⓐ *y*-intercept: 15
      x-intercept: -5

   Ⓑ *y*-intercept: -15
      x-intercept: -5

   Ⓒ *y*-intercept: -15
      x-intercept: -3

   Ⓓ *y*-intercept: 15
      x-intercept: 3

   Ⓔ *y*-intercept: -5
      x-intercept: -15

Quantitative Comparison   **In Exercises 5–8, choose the statement below that is true about the given quantities.**

   Ⓐ   The number in column A is greater.

   Ⓑ   The number in column B is greater.

   Ⓒ   The two numbers are equal.

   Ⓓ   The relationship cannot be determined from the given information.

	Column A	*Column B*
5.	*y*-intercept of $y = x - 6$	*y*-intercept of $-2y = 3x + 12$
6.	*x*-intercept of $y = x + 3$	slope of $5y = 10x + 3$
7.	*y*-intercept of $14x + 7y = 35$	*x*-intercept of $y = 2x + 10$
8.	slope of $y = 12$	*y*-intercept of $16y = 2x - 8$

9. *Multiple Choice*   Which function is represented by the graph shown?

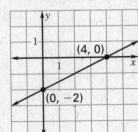

   Ⓐ $-2x - 4y = 8$

   Ⓑ $2x + 4y = 8$

   Ⓒ $2x - 4y = -8$

   Ⓓ $-2x - 4y = -8$

   Ⓔ $2x - 4y = 8$

Algebra 2
Standardized Test Practice Workbook

NAME _____ DATE _____

Standardized Test Practice

For use with pages 91–98

TEST TAKING STRATEGY   **Try to find shortcuts that will help you move through the questions quicker.**

1. *Multiple Choice*   What is the equation of the line that passes through the point $(1, 5)$ and has a slope of -3?

   Ⓐ $y = 3x + 8$ Ⓑ $y = 3x - 2$

   Ⓒ $y = -3x - 8$ Ⓓ $y = -3x + 8$

   Ⓔ $y = -3x + 2$

2. *Multiple Choice*   What is the equation of the line that passes through the point $(-2, -3)$ and has a slope of 4?

   Ⓐ $y = 4x + 5$ Ⓑ $y = 4x + 11$

   Ⓒ $y = -4x + 5$ Ⓓ $y = 4x - 5$

   Ⓔ $y = 4x - 11$

3. *Multiple Choice*   What is the equation of the line that passes through the point $(-1, 7)$ and is parallel to the line $y = -2x - 1$?

   Ⓐ $y = \frac{1}{2}x + \frac{15}{2}$ Ⓑ $y = 2x + 5$

   Ⓒ $y = -\frac{1}{2}x + \frac{13}{2}$ Ⓓ $y = 2x - 9$

   Ⓔ $y = -2x + 5$

4. *Multiple Choice*   What is the equation of the line that passes through the point $(6, -3)$ and is perpendicular to the line $y = \frac{1}{3}x + 4$?

   Ⓐ $y = 3x + 15$ Ⓑ $y = 3x - 15$

   Ⓒ $y = -3x + 15$ Ⓓ $y = \frac{1}{3}x - 5$

   Ⓔ $y = \frac{1}{3}x - 1$

Quantitative Comparison   **In Exercises 5–7, choose the statement below that is true about the given quantities.**

   Ⓐ   The number in column A is greater.

   Ⓑ   The number in column B is greater.

   Ⓒ   The two numbers are equal.

   Ⓓ   The relationship cannot be determined from the given information.

	Column A	Column B
5.	slope of line perpendicular to $y = -3x + 7$	slope of line parallel to $y = 3x - 5$
6.	slope of line parallel to $y = -5x - 11$	slope of line perpendicular to $y = \frac{1}{5}x + \frac{3}{7}$
7.	slope of line parallel to $3y + x = 14$	slope of line perpendicular to $-x + 2y = 15$

8. *Multiple Choice*   The variables x and y vary directly, and $y = 18$ when $x = 36$. Which equation relates the variables?

   Ⓐ $y = 2x$ Ⓑ $y = 36x$

   Ⓒ $y = \frac{1}{36}x$ Ⓓ $y = \frac{1}{2}x$

   Ⓔ $y = 18x$

9. *Multiple Choice*   The variables x and y vary directly, and $y = 42$ when $x = 3$. Which equation relates the variables?

   Ⓐ $y = 14x$ Ⓑ $y = \frac{1}{14}x$

   Ⓒ $y = 3x$ Ⓓ $y = 42x$

   Ⓔ $y = \frac{1}{3}x$

Standardized Test Practice

For use with pages 100–107

TEST TAKING STRATEGY   **You can always return to a more difficult problem later with a fresh perspective.**

1. *Multiple Choice*   If *y* tends to increase as *x* increases on a scatter plot, what is the correlation of the paired data?

   Ⓐ positive
   Ⓑ negative
   Ⓒ relatively no
   Ⓓ undefined
   Ⓔ none of these

2. *Multiple Choice*   What is the correlation represented by the scatter plot shown?

   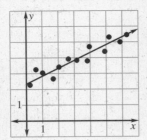

   Ⓐ positive
   Ⓑ negative
   Ⓒ relatively no
   Ⓓ undefined
   Ⓔ none of these

3. *Multiple Choice*   Which is the best-fitting line for the data shown?

x	1	2	3	4	5
y	4.2	3.8	3.5	2.7	2.2

   Ⓐ $y = 0.51x + 4.81$
   Ⓑ $y = -0.051x + 4.8$
   Ⓒ $y = 5.1x + 0.481$
   Ⓓ $y = -0.51x + 4.81$
   Ⓔ $y = -0.0051x + 4.81$

4. *Multi-Step Problem*   The table gives the number *x* of hours per month a company devotes to work safety training and the number *y* of work-hours lost per month due to accidents on the job.

x	1	2	3	4	5	6
y	62	58	50	41	36	33

   a. Draw a scatter plot of the data.

   b. Describe the correlation shown by the scatter plot.

   c. Approximate the best-fitting line for the data.

   d. Using the equation from part (c), predict the number of work-hours lost per month if the company devotes 9 hours per month to safety training.

5. *Multiple Choice*   What is the correlation represented by the scatter plot shown?

   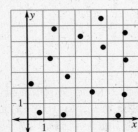

   Ⓐ positive
   Ⓑ negative
   Ⓒ relatively no
   Ⓓ undefined
   Ⓔ none of these

TEST TAKING STRATEGY   **When checking your answer to a question, try using a method different from the one you used to get the answer.**

1. *Multiple Choice*   Which of the ordered pairs is a solution of $2x - 5y \leq 8$?

   Ⓐ $(2, -5)$ Ⓑ $(0, -3)$
   Ⓒ $(-1, -2)$ Ⓓ $(5, 0)$
   Ⓔ $(-2, -5)$

2. *Multiple Choice*   Which of the ordered pairs is a solution of $-x - 3y > -4$?

   Ⓐ $(-3, 2)$ Ⓑ $(2, 2)$
   Ⓒ $(-1, 4)$ Ⓓ $(6, 0)$
   Ⓔ $(0, 9)$

3. *Multiple Choice*   Which of the ordered pairs is *not* a solution of $x < -y + 3$?

   Ⓐ $(-3, 5)$ Ⓑ $(-4, 7)$
   Ⓒ $(6, -7)$ Ⓓ $(-1, 3)$
   Ⓔ $(0, 1)$

4. *Multiple Choice*   Which of the ordered pairs is *not* a solution of $2y \geq 3x - 2$?

   Ⓐ $(-3, -5)$ Ⓑ $(0, 2)$
   Ⓒ $(-2, 0)$ Ⓓ $(2, 2)$
   Ⓔ $(-1, 3)$

5. *Multi-Step Problem*   You have relatives living in both the United States and Canada. You are given a prepaid phone card worth $75. Calls within the continental United States cost $.13 per minute and calls to Canada cost $.62 per minute.

   a. Write a verbal model that represents the number of minutes you can use for calls within the United States and for calls to Canada.

   b. Assign labels using two variables for the verbal model in part (a).

   c. Write an algebraic model based on the labels assigned in part (b).

   d. Graph the inequality in part (c).

   e. *Writing*   Explain why 100 minutes of calls within both the United States and Canada is a possible use of the prepaid phone card, while 80 minutes within the United States and 110 minutes within Canada is not possible.

6. *Multiple Choice*   Which inequality is represented by the graph shown?

   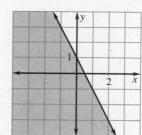

   Ⓐ $y > -2x + 1$
   Ⓑ $y \geq -2x + 1$
   Ⓒ $y < -2x + 1$
   Ⓓ $y \leq -2x + 1$
   Ⓔ $y \neq -2x + 1$

7. *Multiple Choice*   Which inequality is represented by the graph shown?

   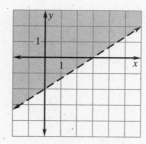

   Ⓐ $y < \frac{2}{3}x - 2$

   Ⓑ $y \leq \frac{2}{3}x - 2$

   Ⓒ $y > \frac{2}{3}x - 2$

   Ⓓ $y \geq \frac{2}{3}x - 2$

   Ⓔ $y \neq \frac{2}{3}x - 2$

Chapter 2

Standardized Test Practice

For use with pages 114–120

TEST TAKING STRATEGY **Spend no more than a few minutes on each question.**

1. **Multiple Choice** If

$$f(x) = \begin{cases} 4x + 1, & \text{if } x < -1 \\ 2x - 3, & \text{if } x \geq -1 \end{cases},$$

what is $f(-1)$?

Ⓐ -5 Ⓑ 3

Ⓒ -1 Ⓓ -3

Ⓔ 5

2. **Multiple Choice** If

$$f(x) = \begin{cases} -2x - 6, & \text{if } x > 2 \\ x - 4, & \text{if } x \leq 2 \end{cases},$$

what is $f(3)$?

Ⓐ -2 Ⓑ -1

Ⓒ -10 Ⓓ -12

Ⓔ 0

3. **Multiple Choice** If

$$f(x) = \begin{cases} -5, & \text{if } -3 < x < 0 \\ 3, & \text{if } 0 \leq x \leq 1, \\ 7, & \text{if } 1 < x < 4 \end{cases}$$

what is $f(1)$?

Ⓐ -5 Ⓑ 1

Ⓒ 0 Ⓓ 7

Ⓔ 3

4. **Multiple Choice** If

$$f(x) = \begin{cases} -x, & \text{if } -1 \leq x \leq 0 \\ x, & \text{if } 0 < x \leq 1, \\ -2x, & \text{if } 1 < x \leq 2 \end{cases}$$

what is $f\left(\frac{1}{2}\right)$?

Ⓐ -1 Ⓑ 2

Ⓒ $\frac{1}{2}$ Ⓓ -2

Ⓔ $-\frac{1}{2}$

Quantitative Comparison **In Exercises 5–9, choose the statement below that is true about the given quantities.**

Ⓐ The number in column A is greater.

Ⓑ The number in column B is greater.

Ⓒ The two numbers are equal.

Ⓓ The relationship cannot be determined from the given information.

	Column A	Column B
5.	$f(-2)$ when $f(x) =$ $\begin{cases} -x + 1, & \text{if } x \geq 0 \\ x - 3, & \text{if } x < 0 \end{cases}$	$f(3)$ when $f(x) =$ $\begin{cases} 2x + 4, & \text{if } x < 3 \\ x + 5, & \text{if } x \geq 3 \end{cases}$
6.	$f(0)$ when $f(x) =$ $\begin{cases} 5x, & \text{if } x < 2 \\ 3x + 1, & \text{if } x \geq 2 \end{cases}$	$f(-4)$ when $f(x) =$ $\begin{cases} x + 4, & \text{if } x \geq -4 \\ 2x + 7, & \text{if } x < -4 \end{cases}$
7.	$f(1)$ when $f(x) =$ $\begin{cases} -3x + 1, & \text{if } x > 2 \\ 3 - x, & \text{if } x \leq 2 \end{cases}$	$f(5)$ when $f(x) =$ $\begin{cases} -6x + 1, & \text{if } x \leq 7 \\ 4x - 1, & \text{if } x > 7 \end{cases}$
8.	$f(-4)$ when $f(x) =$ $\begin{cases} \frac{1}{2}x + 1, & \text{if } x < 0 \\ x - 1, & \text{if } x \geq 0 \end{cases}$	$f(-6)$ when $f(x) =$ $\begin{cases} x - 4, & \text{if } x < -6 \\ \frac{2}{3}x + 5, & \text{if } x \geq -6 \end{cases}$
9.	$f(7)$ when $f(x) =$ $\begin{cases} \frac{3}{4}x + 2, & \text{if } x < 5 \\ -2x - 4, & \text{if } x \geq 5 \end{cases}$	$f(10)$ when $f(x) =$ $\begin{cases} \frac{1}{5}x - 20, & \text{if } x \geq -8 \\ \frac{2}{5}x + 12, & \text{if } x < -8 \end{cases}$

10. Which function is represented by the graph shown?

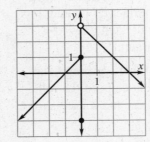

Ⓐ $f(x) = \begin{cases} x + 1, \text{if } x \leq 0 \\ x + 3, \text{if } x > 0 \end{cases}$

Ⓑ $f(x) = \begin{cases} x + 1, \text{if } x < 0 \\ x - 3, \text{if } x \geq 0 \end{cases}$

Ⓒ $f(x) = \begin{cases} x - 1, \text{if } x \geq 0 \\ x + 3, \text{if } x < 0 \end{cases}$

Ⓓ $f(x) = \begin{cases} x + 1, \text{if } x \leq 0 \\ -x + 3, \text{if } x > 0 \end{cases}$

Ⓔ $f(x) = \begin{cases} x + 1, \text{if } x < 0 \\ -x + 3, \text{if } x \geq 0 \end{cases}$

Algebra 2
Standardized Test Practice Workbook

NAME _____ DATE _____

Standardized Test Practice

For use with pages 122–128

TEST TAKING STRATEGY   Do not panic if you run out of time before answering all of the questions. You can still receive a high score on a standardized test without answering every question.

1. *Multiple Choice*   Which function is represented by the graph shown?

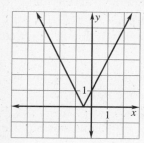

Ⓐ $y = |2x - 1|$

Ⓑ $y = |2x + 1|$

Ⓒ $y = |-2x + 1|$

Ⓓ $y = |-2x| - 1$

Ⓔ $y = |2x| - 1$

2. *Multiple Choice*   Which function is represented by the graph shown?

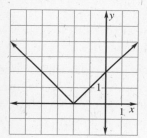

Ⓐ $y = |x - 2|$

Ⓑ $y = |x| + 2$

Ⓒ $y = |-x + 2|$

Ⓓ $y = -|x| + 2$

Ⓔ $y = |-x - 2|$

3. *Multiple Choice*   Which function is represented by the graph shown?

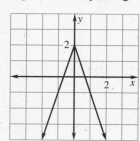

Ⓐ $y = |3x + 2|$

Ⓑ $y = |2 - 3x|$

Ⓒ $y = -|3x| + 2$

Ⓓ $y = |-3x + 2|$

Ⓔ $y = |3x| + 2$

Quantitative Comparison   **In Exercises 4–7, choose the statement below that is true about the given quantities.**

Ⓐ   The number in column A is greater.

Ⓑ   The number in column B is greater.

Ⓒ   The two numbers are equal.

Ⓓ   The relationship cannot be determined from the given information.

	Column A	Column B
4.	$y = 3|x| + 4$ when $x = -2$	$y = |x - 11|$ when $x = 1$
5.	$y = |x + 4|$ when $x = 0$	$y = |-2x|$ when $x = 2$
6.	$y = -|x - 5|$ when $x = 12$	$y = -|-x - 2| - 6$ when $x = 11$
7.	$y = |0.5x - 8|$ when $y = 0$	$y = |0.25x - 5|$ when $y = 0$

8. *Multiple Choice*   Which statement is true about the graph of the function $y = |x - 7| + 3$?

Ⓐ   Its vertex is at $(0, 10)$.

Ⓑ   Its vertex is at $(-7, 3)$.

Ⓒ   Its vertex is at $(3, 7)$.

Ⓓ   Its vertex is at $(10, 0)$.

Ⓔ   Its vertex is at $(7, 3)$.

NAME _____ DATE _____

Standardized Test Practice

For use with pages 139–145

TEST TAKING STRATEGY   **If you find yourself spending too much time on one question and getting frustrated, move on to the next question.**

1. *Multiple Choice*   Which ordered pair is a solution of the following system of linear equations?

$$x - 3y = 5$$
$$-x + 5y = -7$$

Ⓐ $(2, 1)$ Ⓑ $(2, -1)$
Ⓒ $(1, 2)$ Ⓓ $(-1, 2)$
Ⓔ $(2, 2)$

2. *Multiple Choice*   Which ordered pair is a solution of the following system of linear equations?

$$5x + 3y = 4$$
$$2x - y = -5$$

Ⓐ $(3, 1)$ Ⓑ $(3, -1)$
Ⓒ $(-1, 3)$ Ⓓ $(-3, 1)$
Ⓔ $(3, 2)$

3. *Multiple Choice*   How many solutions does the following system have?

$$3x - y = -6$$
$$3x - y = 14$$

Ⓐ 0   Ⓑ 1
Ⓒ 2   Ⓓ 3
Ⓔ infinitely many

4. *Multiple Choice*   How many solutions does the following system have?

$$-2x - 4y = 8$$
$$3x + 6y = -12$$

Ⓐ 0   Ⓑ 1
Ⓒ 2   Ⓓ 3
Ⓔ infinitely many

5. *Multi-Step Problem*   You are choosing between two electricity providers. The Zap Electric Company charges $0.06 per kilowatt hour plus a $6.55 monthly service fee. The Bolt Electric Company charges $0.12 per kilowatt hour plus a $2.83 monthly service fee.

   a. Let x represent the number of kilowatt hours you use in one month, and let y represent the total cost of your electric service. Write the two equations representing the cost of each company's service for one month.

   b. Graph the two equations from part (a) on the same graph.

   c. Estimate the coordinates of the point where the two graphs intersect.

   d. *Critical Thinking*   Explain which company to choose if you want to keep your cost at a minimum and you use an average of 82 kilowatt hours per month.

6. *Multiple Choice*   Which system of linear equations is shown in the graph?

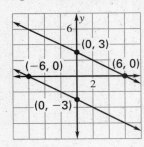

Ⓐ $x - 2y = -1$
     $2x + 5y = 7$

Ⓑ $\frac{1}{2}x + y = 3$
     $x + 2y = -6$

Ⓒ $-3x - 4y = 2$
     $4x + 5y = -1$

Ⓓ $\frac{1}{5}x + \frac{3}{4}y = 1$
     $\frac{2}{3}x - \frac{1}{6}y = 2$

Ⓔ $-6x + 3y = 15$
     $4x - 2y = -10$

NAME _____ DATE _____

Standardized Test Practice

For use with pages 148–155

TEST TAKING STRATEGY   **If you get stuck on a question, look at the answer choices for clues.**

1. *Multiple Choice*   Which ordered pair is a solution of the following system of linear equations?

$$x + 2y = -1$$
$$2x - y = 13$$

  Ⓐ $(5, 3)$ Ⓑ $(-3, -5)$

  Ⓒ $(5, -3)$ Ⓓ $(-5, 3)$

  Ⓔ $(3, 5)$

2. *Multiple Choice*   Which ordered pair is a solution of the following system of linear equations?

$$-3x - 5y = -23$$
$$2x - 4y = -14$$

  Ⓐ $(1, 4)$ Ⓑ $(4, -1)$

  Ⓒ $(1, -4)$ Ⓓ $(-4, 1)$

  Ⓔ $(-1, 4)$

3. *Multiple Choice*   Which ordered pair is a solution of the following system of linear equations?

$$5x + 6y = -9$$
$$-x - 8y = -5$$

  Ⓐ $(1, 3)$ Ⓑ $(3, -1)$

  Ⓒ $(-3, 1)$ Ⓓ $(-3, -1)$

  Ⓔ $(1, -3)$

Quantitative Comparison   **In Exercises 4–6, choose the statement below that is true about the given quantities.**

  Ⓐ   The number in column A is greater.

  Ⓑ   The number in column B is greater.

  Ⓒ   The two numbers are equal.

  Ⓓ   The relationship cannot be determined from the given information.

	Column A	Column B
4.	the x-coordinate of the solution of: $3x - 2y = 14$ $2x + 5y = 3$	-4
5.	5	the y-coordinate of the solution of: $x - 3y = -13$ $2x + y = 16$
6.	the x-coordinate of the solution of: $-2x + y = 3$ $6x - 3y = -9$	the y-coordinate of the solution of: $5x - 2y = 1$ $8x + 5y = 18$

7. *Multiple Choice*   You sold 52 boxes of candy for your marching band fundraiser. The large size box costs $3.50 each and the small size box costs $1.75 each. If you sold $112.00 worth of candy, how many boxes of each size did you sell?

  Ⓐ   9 large boxes and 43 small boxes

  Ⓑ   10 large boxes and 42 small boxes

  Ⓒ   11 large boxes and 41 small boxes

  Ⓓ   12 large boxes and 40 small boxes

  Ⓔ   13 large boxes and 39 small boxes

Chapter 3

Standardized Test Practice

For use with pages 156–162

TEST TAKING STRATEGY   **The best way to prepare for a standardized test is to keep up with your day-to-day studies.**

1. *Multiple Choice*   Which ordered pair is *not* a solution of the following system of linear inequalities?

   $x < 4$

   $y \leq x$

   Ⓐ $(2, -3)$ Ⓑ $(-1, 2)$

   Ⓒ $(1, -1)$ Ⓓ $(3, 3)$

   Ⓔ $(3, 4)$

2. *Multiple Choice*   Which ordered pair is *not* a solution of the following system of linear inequalities?

   $y \leq -x + 4$

   $y \geq \dfrac{1}{2}x - 2$

   Ⓐ $(0, 2)$ Ⓑ $(1, 3)$

   Ⓒ $(-2, 2)$ Ⓓ $(3, 2)$

   Ⓔ $(-1, -1)$

3. *Multiple Choice*   Which ordered pair is *not* a solution of the following system of linear inequalities?

   $x \geq -1$

   $y < 3$

   $y \geq 2x - 1$

   Ⓐ $(0, 1)$ Ⓑ $(1, -2)$

   Ⓒ $(0, 0)$ Ⓓ $(1, 2)$

   Ⓔ $(-1, 1)$

Quantitative Comparison   **In Exercises 4 and 5, choose the statement below that is true about the given quantities.**

   Ⓐ The number in column A is greater.

   Ⓑ The number in column B is greater.

   Ⓒ The two numbers are equal.

   Ⓓ The relationship cannot be determined from the given information.

	Column A	Column B
4.	x-coordinate in any solution of: $y \leq -2x + 6$ $y > 0$	4
5.	0	x-coordinate in any solution of: $x \leq 5$ $y < \dfrac{3}{5}x - 3$

6. *Multiple Choice*   Which system of linear inequalities is shown in the graph?

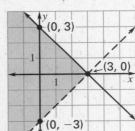

   Ⓐ $y < -x + 3$
       $y \geq x - 3$

   Ⓑ $y > -x + 3$
       $y < x - 3$

   Ⓒ $y \leq -x + 3$
       $y > x - 3$

   Ⓓ $y \leq -x + 3$
       $y \geq x - 3$

   Ⓔ $y < -x + 3$
       $y > x - 3$

Chapter 3

NAME _____ DATE _____

Standardized Test Practice

For use with pages 163–169

TEST TAKING STRATEGY   **When checking your answer to a question, try using a method different from the one you used to get the answer.**

1. *Multiple Choice*   What is the maximum value of the objective function $C = 2x + 3y$ subject to the following constraints?

    $x \geq 0$

    $y \geq 0$

    $y \leq -2x + 6$

    Ⓐ 0   Ⓑ 3

    Ⓒ 6   Ⓓ 18

    Ⓔ 24

2. *Multiple Choice*   What is the minimum value of the objective function $C = 5x + 2y$ subject to the following constraints?

    $x \geq 0$

    $y \leq 0$

    $y \geq \dfrac{2}{3}x - 4$

    Ⓐ −8   Ⓑ −4

    Ⓒ 0   Ⓓ 6

    Ⓔ 30

3. *Multiple Choice*   Given the feasible region shown, which is the maximum value of the objective function $C = 6x + y$?

    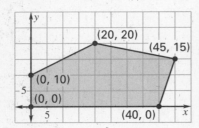

    Ⓐ 0

    Ⓑ 10

    Ⓒ 140

    Ⓓ 240

    Ⓔ 285

Quantitative Comparison   **In Exercises 4–6, choose the statement below that is true about the given quantities using the objective function $C = 4x + 5y$ subject to the following constraints.**

   $x \geq 0$

   $y \geq 0$

   $y \leq -x + 3$

   $y \geq x$

Ⓐ   The number in column A is greater.

Ⓑ   The number in column B is greater.

Ⓒ   The two numbers are equal.

Ⓓ   The relationship cannot be determined from the given information.

	Column A	Column B
4.	maximum value of C	6
5.	minimum value of C	0
6.	maximum value of C	7.5

7. *Multiple Choice*   Given the feasible region shown, which is the minimum value of the objective function $C = 4x - 3y$?

    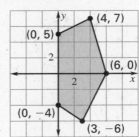

    Ⓐ −15

    Ⓑ −5

    Ⓒ 0

    Ⓓ 12

    Ⓔ 30

Standardized Test Practice

For use with pages 170–176

TEST TAKING STRATEGY **The mathematical portion of a standardized test is based on concepts and skills taught in high school mathematics courses.**

1. *Multiple Choice* Which linear equation is graphed below?

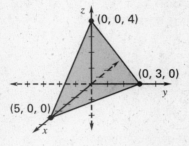

(0, 0, 4)

(0, 3, 0)

(5, 0, 0)

Ⓐ $12x + 20y + 15z = -60$

Ⓑ $12x + 20y - 15z = 60$

Ⓒ $12x - 20y + 15z = 60$

Ⓓ $12x + 20y + 15z = 60$

Ⓔ $12x - 20y - 15z = -60$

2. *Multiple Choice* Which linear equation is graphed below?

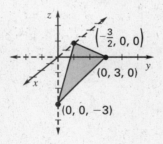

$\left(-\frac{3}{2}, 0, 0\right)$

(0, 3, 0)

(0, 0, -3)

Ⓐ $2x - y - z = -3$

Ⓑ $2x + y - z = 3$

Ⓒ $2x - y + z = -3$

Ⓓ $2x - y + z = -3$

Ⓔ $2x + y + z = -3$

3. *Multiple Choice* At which point does the graph of $12x + 4y - 6z = 12$ cross the x-axis?

Ⓐ (0, 3, 0)   Ⓑ (−1, 0, 0)

Ⓒ (12, 0, 0)   Ⓓ (0, 0, 2)

Ⓔ (1, 0, 0)

4. *Multiple Choice* At which point does the graph of $7x - 14y - 4z = -28$ cross the z-axis?

Ⓐ (0, 0, 7)   Ⓑ (4, 0, 0)

Ⓒ (−4, 0, 0)   Ⓓ (0, 2, 0)

Ⓔ (0, 0, −7)

Quantitative Comparison **In Exercises 5 and 6, choose the statement below that is true about the given quantities.**

Ⓐ The number in column A is greater.

Ⓑ The number in column B is greater.

Ⓒ The two numbers are equal.

Ⓓ The relationship cannot be determined from the given information.

	Column A	Column B
5.	$f(x, y) =$ $\frac{2}{5}(15 + x - 3y),$ $f(1, 2)$	$f(x, y) =$ $\frac{2}{5}(15 + x - 3y),$ $f(7, 4)$
6.	$f(x, y) =$ $\frac{1}{6}(24 - 2x + 5y),$ $f(1, 2)$	$f(x, y) =$ $\frac{1}{6}(24 - 2x + 5y),$ $f(4, 3)$

Algebra 2
Standardized Test Practice Workbook

Chapter 3

Standardized Test Practice

For use with pages 177–183

TEST TAKING STRATEGY   **If you start to get tense during a test, put your pencil down and take some deep breaths. This may help you regain control.**

1. *Multiple Choice* Which ordered triple is a solution of the following linear system?

$$x - y + z = 5$$
$$x + y + z = 7$$
$$x + y - z = -1$$

 Ⓐ $(2, 1, -4)$ Ⓑ $(2, -1, 4)$

 Ⓒ $(2, 1, 4)$ Ⓓ $(-2, -1, 4)$

 Ⓔ $(-2, 1, 4)$

2. *Multiple Choice* Which ordered triple is a solution of the following linear system?

$$2x + 3y - z = 4$$
$$x - 3y + 2z = -3$$
$$3x + y - z = 5$$

 Ⓐ $(2, 0, -1)$ Ⓑ $(2, -1, 0)$

 Ⓒ $(1, 0, 2)$ Ⓓ $(-1, 0, 2)$

 Ⓔ $(1, 0, -2)$

3. *Multiple Choice* How many solutions does a system of linear equations in three variables have if in solving the system you correctly obtain the equation $-2 = -2$?

 Ⓐ 0   Ⓑ 1

 Ⓒ 2   Ⓓ 3

 Ⓔ infinitely many

4. *Multiple Choice* Which ordered triple is a solution of the following linear system?

$$-4x - 3y + 2z = -19$$
$$3x + y + 3z = 6$$
$$5x - 2y + 4z = 0$$

 Ⓐ $(2, -3, -1)$ Ⓑ $(2, 3, -1)$

 Ⓒ $(-2, 3, 1)$ Ⓓ $(-2, -3, 1)$

 Ⓔ $(-2, -3, -1)$

5. *Multi-Step Problem* You have \$12 to spend on picking 9 pints of three different types of berries at the Berry-Fine Berry Field. The strawberries cost \$1.20 per pint, the blackberries cost \$2.00 per pint, and the raspberries cost \$1.40 per pint. You want twice as many strawberries as the other two kinds combined.

   a. Write a system of equations to represent the given information.

   b. How many pints of each type of berry should you buy?

   c. *Critical Thinking* Explain if it's possible to increase the amount of pints for each type of berry by 25% if the Berry Farm offers a 25% discount and still spend within your \$12 limit.

6. *Multiple Choice* How many solutions does a system of linear equations in three variables have if in solving the system you correctly obtain the equation $0 = 7$?

 Ⓐ 0   Ⓑ 1

 Ⓒ 2   Ⓓ 3

 Ⓔ infinitely many

Chapter 3

NAME _____ DATE _____

Standardized Test Practice

For use with pages 199–206

TEST TAKING STRATEGY   **If you get stuck on a question, look at the answer choices for clues.**

1. *Multiple Choice*   Which matrix equals

$\begin{bmatrix} -1 & 2 \\ 8 & 6 \end{bmatrix} + \begin{bmatrix} 4 & -6 \\ -3 & -2 \end{bmatrix}$?

Ⓐ $\begin{bmatrix} 5 & 8 \\ 11 & 8 \end{bmatrix}$ Ⓑ $\begin{bmatrix} 3 & 4 \\ 5 & 4 \end{bmatrix}$

Ⓒ $\begin{bmatrix} 3 & -4 \\ 5 & 4 \end{bmatrix}$ Ⓓ $\begin{bmatrix} -3 & 4 \\ 5 & 4 \end{bmatrix}$

Ⓔ $\begin{bmatrix} -5 & -8 \\ -11 & -8 \end{bmatrix}$

2. *Multiple Choice*   Which matrix equals

$3\left(\begin{bmatrix} 1 \\ -3 \end{bmatrix} + \begin{bmatrix} -6 \\ 2 \end{bmatrix} \right)$?

Ⓐ $\begin{bmatrix} -\frac{5}{3} \\ -\frac{1}{3} \end{bmatrix}$ Ⓑ $\begin{bmatrix} 15 \\ 3 \end{bmatrix}$

Ⓒ $\begin{bmatrix} -15 \\ -3 \end{bmatrix}$ Ⓓ $\begin{bmatrix} 15 \\ -3 \end{bmatrix}$

Ⓔ $\begin{bmatrix} \frac{5}{3} \\ -\frac{1}{3} \end{bmatrix}$

3. *Multiple Choice*   Which matrix equals

$2\begin{bmatrix} 2 & 0 \\ -3 & 4 \end{bmatrix} - 3\begin{bmatrix} -6 & -2 \\ 1 & 1 \end{bmatrix}$?

Ⓐ $\begin{bmatrix} -14 & -2 \\ 3 & 5 \end{bmatrix}$ Ⓑ $\begin{bmatrix} -22 & 6 \\ 9 & -5 \end{bmatrix}$

Ⓒ $\begin{bmatrix} 14 & 2 \\ -3 & -5 \end{bmatrix}$ Ⓓ $\begin{bmatrix} 22 & -6 \\ 9 & -5 \end{bmatrix}$

Ⓔ $\begin{bmatrix} 22 & 6 \\ -9 & 5 \end{bmatrix}$

4. *Multi-Step Problem*   The matrices show the number of gallons of gasoline sold and the average price per gallon (in dollars) for the three different grades of gasoline.

	1998 (A)		1999 (B)	
	Gallons	Price	Gallons	Price
Supreme	862,496	$1.45	742,883	$1.53
Plus	1,026,211	$1.32	1,167,129	$1.42
Regular	1,128,453	$1.26	1,516,084	$1.33

a. Calculate $B - A$. How many more (or fewer) gallons of supreme gas were sold in 1999 than in 1998? How much more (or less) did regular gas cost in 1999 than in 1998?

b. Calculate $B + A$. During the years 1998 and 1999, which grade of gasoline sold the most? Which grade sold the least?

c. Does the matrix in part (b) give you information about how much money was made in gasoline sales during 1998 and 1999?

d. *Critical Thinking*   Explain whether or not you can conclude from the matrix in part (a) that the less you raise the price per gallon the more gasoline you will sell.

5. *Multiple Choice*   Which matrix equals

$\begin{bmatrix} -\frac{6}{2} & \frac{2}{5} \\ -\frac{4}{8} & \frac{12}{3} \end{bmatrix}$?

Ⓐ $\begin{bmatrix} 3 & -0.4 \\ 0.5 & -4 \end{bmatrix}$ Ⓑ $\begin{bmatrix} -3 & 0.4 \\ -0.5 & 4 \end{bmatrix}$

Ⓒ $\begin{bmatrix} -3 & 0.4 \\ -0.5 & -4 \end{bmatrix}$ Ⓓ $\begin{bmatrix} -3 & -0.4 \\ -0.5 & -4 \end{bmatrix}$

Ⓔ $\begin{bmatrix} 3 & 0.4 \\ 0.5 & 4 \end{bmatrix}$

Algebra 2
Standardized Test Practice Workbook

Standardized Test Practice

For use with pages 208–213

TEST TAKING STRATEGY **Draw an arrow on your test booklet next to questions that you do not answer. This will enable you to find the questions quickly when you go back.**

1. *Multiple Choice* If A is a 4×5 matrix and B is a 5×4 matrix, what are the dimensions of BA?

   Ⓐ 4×4 Ⓑ 5×5

   Ⓒ 4×5 Ⓓ 5×4

   Ⓔ BA is not defined

2. *Multiple Choice* If A is a 1×3 matrix and B is a 3×1 matrix, what are the dimensions of AB?

   Ⓐ 1×1 Ⓑ 3×3

   Ⓒ 1×3 Ⓓ 3×1

   Ⓔ AB is not defined

3. *Multiple Choice* What is the product of $\begin{bmatrix} -2 & 3 \\ 1 & -4 \end{bmatrix}$ and $\begin{bmatrix} 0 & 2 \\ 3 & -6 \end{bmatrix}$?

   Ⓐ $\begin{bmatrix} 6 & -8 \\ -24 & 27 \end{bmatrix}$ Ⓑ $\begin{bmatrix} 8 & -12 \\ 2 & 26 \end{bmatrix}$

   Ⓒ $\begin{bmatrix} 2 & -8 \\ -12 & 33 \end{bmatrix}$ Ⓓ $\begin{bmatrix} 9 & -22 \\ -12 & 26 \end{bmatrix}$

   Ⓔ $\begin{bmatrix} 9 & 22 \\ 12 & -26 \end{bmatrix}$

Quantitative Comparison **In Exercises 4–6, choose the statement below that is true about the given quantities.**

   Ⓐ The number in column A is greater.

   Ⓑ The number in column B is greater.

   Ⓒ The two numbers are equal.

   Ⓓ The relationship cannot be determined from the given information.

	Column A	Column B
4.	Number of rows in the matrix $\begin{bmatrix} 3 \\ 2 \\ 1 \end{bmatrix}$	Number of columns in the matrix $\begin{bmatrix} 2 & -4 & 0 \\ -3 & 6 & 5 \end{bmatrix}$
5.	The value of x in $\begin{bmatrix} 2 & 4 \\ 2 & 1 \end{bmatrix}\begin{bmatrix} 1 \\ 0 \end{bmatrix} = \begin{bmatrix} x \\ 2 \end{bmatrix}$.	The value of y in $\begin{bmatrix} -1 & 3 \\ 0 & 4 \end{bmatrix}\begin{bmatrix} -3 \\ -1 \end{bmatrix} = \begin{bmatrix} 0 \\ y \end{bmatrix}$.
6.	The value of x in $\begin{bmatrix} -2 & 3 \end{bmatrix}\begin{bmatrix} 1 & 0 & 4 \\ 2 & 4 & -1 \end{bmatrix} = \begin{bmatrix} 4 & x & -11 \end{bmatrix}$.	The value of y in $\begin{bmatrix} 1 & 0 & 2 \\ 1 & 3 & -2 \end{bmatrix}\begin{bmatrix} 5 \\ 1 \\ 0 \end{bmatrix} = \begin{bmatrix} y \\ 8 \end{bmatrix}$.

7. *Multiple Choice* What is $A(B + C)$ if $A = \begin{bmatrix} 3 & -2 \\ -6 & -1 \end{bmatrix}$, $B = \begin{bmatrix} -1 \\ 0 \end{bmatrix}$ and $C = \begin{bmatrix} 5 \\ 2 \end{bmatrix}$?

   Ⓐ $\begin{bmatrix} -8 \\ 26 \end{bmatrix}$ Ⓑ $\begin{bmatrix} 4 \\ -14 \end{bmatrix}$

   Ⓒ $\begin{bmatrix} 8 \\ 26 \end{bmatrix}$ Ⓓ $\begin{bmatrix} -4 \\ 14 \end{bmatrix}$

   Ⓔ $\begin{bmatrix} 8 \\ -26 \end{bmatrix}$

Chapter 4

TEST TAKING STRATEGY   **Some college entrance exams allow the optional use of calculators. If you do use a calculator, make sure it is one you are familiar with and have used before.**

1. *Multiple Choice*   What is the determinant of $\begin{bmatrix} 1 & 2 \\ -3 & 6 \end{bmatrix}$?

   Ⓐ 0   Ⓑ -12
   Ⓒ 12   Ⓓ -36
   Ⓔ 36

2. *Multiple Choice*   What is the determinant of $\begin{bmatrix} 4 & -5 \\ -8 & -3 \end{bmatrix}$?

   Ⓐ 38   Ⓑ -52
   Ⓒ -38 Ⓓ 52
   Ⓔ -17

3. *Multiple Choice*   What is the determinant of $\begin{bmatrix} 2 & -1 & 3 \\ 0 & 4 & 1 \\ -6 & 2 & -4 \end{bmatrix}$?

   Ⓐ -42 Ⓑ 30
   Ⓒ -30 Ⓓ 106
   Ⓔ 42

Quantitative Comparison   **In Exercises 4–6, choose the statement below that is true about the given quantities.**

   Ⓐ The number in column A is greater.
   Ⓑ The number in column B is greater.
   Ⓒ The two numbers are equal.
   Ⓓ The relationship cannot be determined from the given information.

	Column A	Column B
4.	$\det \begin{bmatrix} 2 & 0 \\ -5 & -4 \end{bmatrix}$	$\det \begin{bmatrix} 1 & 8 \\ 2 & 7 \end{bmatrix}$
5.	$\det \begin{bmatrix} 4 & -1 & 1 \\ 0 & 3 & -2 \\ 6 & 1 & 5 \end{bmatrix}$	$\det \begin{bmatrix} 6 & 1 & 2 \\ -1 & -1 & 4 \\ 3 & -1 & -2 \end{bmatrix}$
6.	The area of a triangle with vertices $(5, 2)$, $(-6, 1)$, and $(-4, -3)$	The area of a triangle with vertices $(10, -4)$, $(6, 1)$, and $(-5, 3)$

7. What is the area of the triangle in square units?

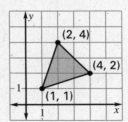

(2, 4)
(4, 2)
(1, 1)

   Ⓐ 4   Ⓑ 8
   Ⓒ 12   Ⓓ 16
   Ⓔ 20

NAME _____ DATE _____

Standardized Test Practice

For use with pages 223–229

TEST TAKING STRATEGY   **If you start to get tense during a test, put your pencil down and take some deep breaths. This may help you regain control.**

1. *Multiple Choice* What is the inverse of $\begin{bmatrix} 8 & -3 \\ 5 & -2 \end{bmatrix}$?

Ⓐ $\begin{bmatrix} 2 & 3 \\ 5 & 8 \end{bmatrix}$ Ⓑ $\begin{bmatrix} 2 & -3 \\ 5 & -8 \end{bmatrix}$

Ⓒ $\begin{bmatrix} 3 & -8 \\ 2 & -5 \end{bmatrix}$ Ⓓ $\begin{bmatrix} -2 & -3 \\ 5 & 8 \end{bmatrix}$

Ⓔ $\begin{bmatrix} -2 & 5 \\ -3 & 8 \end{bmatrix}$

2. *Multiple Choice* What is the inverse of $\begin{bmatrix} -5 & 4 \\ -1 & 1 \end{bmatrix}$?

Ⓐ $\begin{bmatrix} 5 & -4 \\ 1 & -1 \end{bmatrix}$ Ⓑ $\begin{bmatrix} -1 & 4 \\ -1 & 5 \end{bmatrix}$

Ⓒ $\begin{bmatrix} 1 & 4 \\ -1 & -5 \end{bmatrix}$ Ⓓ $\begin{bmatrix} 1 & -4 \\ 1 & -5 \end{bmatrix}$

Ⓔ $\begin{bmatrix} -1 & -4 \\ 1 & 5 \end{bmatrix}$

3. *Multiple Choice* Which matrix has *no* inverse?

Ⓐ $\begin{bmatrix} -3 & 6 \\ -1 & -2 \end{bmatrix}$ Ⓑ $\begin{bmatrix} 3 & -6 \\ 1 & 2 \end{bmatrix}$

Ⓒ $\begin{bmatrix} 3 & 6 \\ -1 & 2 \end{bmatrix}$ Ⓓ $\begin{bmatrix} -3 & -6 \\ -1 & 2 \end{bmatrix}$

Ⓔ $\begin{bmatrix} 3 & -6 \\ -1 & 2 \end{bmatrix}$

4. *Multiple Choice* What is the solution of $\begin{bmatrix} 2 & 1 \\ 4 & 3 \end{bmatrix} X = \begin{bmatrix} -1 \\ 3 \end{bmatrix}$?

Ⓐ $\begin{bmatrix} 3 \\ 5 \end{bmatrix}$ Ⓑ $\begin{bmatrix} 5 \\ 3 \end{bmatrix}$ Ⓒ $\begin{bmatrix} 3 \\ -5 \end{bmatrix}$

Ⓓ $\begin{bmatrix} -3 \\ 5 \end{bmatrix}$ Ⓔ $\begin{bmatrix} -5 \\ 3 \end{bmatrix}$

Quantitative Comparison   **In Exercises 5–7, choose the statement below that is true about the given quantities.**

Ⓐ   The number in column A is greater.

Ⓑ   The number in column B is greater.

Ⓒ   The two numbers are equal.

Ⓓ   The relationship cannot be determined from the given information.

Column A	*Column B*
5. The value of x in the inverse of $A = \begin{bmatrix} 5 & 13 \\ 2 & 5 \end{bmatrix}$; $A^{-1} = \begin{bmatrix} x & 13 \\ 2 & -5 \end{bmatrix}$.	The value of y in the inverse of $B = \begin{bmatrix} 3 & -7 \\ -2 & 5 \end{bmatrix}$; $B^{-1} = \begin{bmatrix} y & 7 \\ 2 & 3 \end{bmatrix}$.
6. The value of x in the inverse of $A = \begin{bmatrix} 13 & -6 \\ 2 & -1 \end{bmatrix}$; $A^{-1} = \begin{bmatrix} 1 & -6 \\ x & -13 \end{bmatrix}$.	The value of y in the inverse of $B = \begin{bmatrix} 3 & 2 \\ -10 & -7 \end{bmatrix}$; $B^{-1} = \begin{bmatrix} 7 & y \\ -10 & -3 \end{bmatrix}$.
7. The value of x in $\begin{bmatrix} -1 & 4 \\ 6 & 2 \end{bmatrix}\begin{bmatrix} 1 \\ x \end{bmatrix} = \begin{bmatrix} -17 \\ -2 \end{bmatrix}$.	The value of y in $\begin{bmatrix} 4 & 0 \\ 3 & 5 \end{bmatrix}\begin{bmatrix} y \\ -3 \end{bmatrix} = \begin{bmatrix} 20 \\ 0 \end{bmatrix}$.

Chapter 4

Algebra 2
Standardized Test Practice Workbook

Standardized Test Practice

For use with pages 230–236

TEST TAKING STRATEGY If you use the same method to find and check an answer, you may make the same mistake twice.

1. **Multiple Choice** Which system of linear equations is represented by the matrix equation

$$\begin{bmatrix} 3 & -2 \\ -4 & 1 \end{bmatrix}\begin{bmatrix} x \\ y \end{bmatrix} = \begin{bmatrix} 10 \\ 7 \end{bmatrix}?$$

Ⓐ $3x - 2x = 10$
$-4y + y = 7$

Ⓑ $3x - 4y = 10$
$-2x + y = 7$

Ⓒ $3x + y = 7$
$-4x - 2y = 10$

Ⓓ $3x - 2y = 10$
$-4x + y = 7$

Ⓔ $3x - 2y = 7$
$-4x + y = 10$

2. **Multiple Choice** Which matrix equation is used to solve the linear system

$$-2x + 5y = -4$$
$$6x - y = 12 \quad ?$$

Ⓐ $\begin{bmatrix} -2 & 5 \\ 6 & -1 \end{bmatrix}\begin{bmatrix} x \\ y \end{bmatrix} = \begin{bmatrix} -4 \\ 12 \end{bmatrix}$

Ⓑ $\begin{bmatrix} -2 & 6 \\ 5 & -1 \end{bmatrix}\begin{bmatrix} x \\ y \end{bmatrix} = \begin{bmatrix} -4 \\ 12 \end{bmatrix}$

Ⓒ $\begin{bmatrix} -2 & 6 \\ 5 & -1 \end{bmatrix}\begin{bmatrix} y \\ x \end{bmatrix} = \begin{bmatrix} -4 \\ 12 \end{bmatrix}$

Ⓓ $\begin{bmatrix} -2 & 5 \\ 6 & -1 \end{bmatrix}\begin{bmatrix} y \\ x \end{bmatrix} = \begin{bmatrix} 4 \\ -12 \end{bmatrix}$

Ⓔ $\begin{bmatrix} -2 & -1 \\ 6 & 5 \end{bmatrix}\begin{bmatrix} x \\ y \end{bmatrix} = \begin{bmatrix} -4 \\ 12 \end{bmatrix}$

3. **Multiple Choice** Which inverse matrix can be used to solve the linear system

$$-3x - y = -3$$
$$5x + 2y = 4 \quad ?$$

Ⓐ $\begin{bmatrix} -2 & -1 \\ 5 & 3 \end{bmatrix}$

Ⓑ $\begin{bmatrix} -2 & 1 \\ -5 & 3 \end{bmatrix}$

Ⓒ $\begin{bmatrix} 2 & 1 \\ 5 & 3 \end{bmatrix}$

Ⓓ $\begin{bmatrix} 2 & 1 \\ -5 & -3 \end{bmatrix}$

Ⓔ $\begin{bmatrix} -2 & -1 \\ -5 & -3 \end{bmatrix}$

4. **Multiple Choice** Which matrix is the solution matrix for the linear system

$$4x - 2y = -10$$
$$-5x - 6y = -13 \quad ?$$

Ⓐ $\begin{bmatrix} 1 \\ 3 \end{bmatrix}$ Ⓑ $\begin{bmatrix} 3 \\ -1 \end{bmatrix}$ Ⓒ $\begin{bmatrix} -1 \\ -3 \end{bmatrix}$

Ⓓ $\begin{bmatrix} 1 \\ -3 \end{bmatrix}$ Ⓔ $\begin{bmatrix} -1 \\ 3 \end{bmatrix}$

5. **Multiple Choice** Which matrix is the solution matrix for the linear system

$$-x + 5y = -23$$
$$4x - 2y = 20 \quad ?$$

Ⓐ $\begin{bmatrix} -3 \\ 4 \end{bmatrix}$ Ⓑ $\begin{bmatrix} 3 \\ 4 \end{bmatrix}$ Ⓒ $\begin{bmatrix} 3 \\ -4 \end{bmatrix}$

Ⓓ $\begin{bmatrix} -3 \\ -4 \end{bmatrix}$ Ⓔ $\begin{bmatrix} -4 \\ 3 \end{bmatrix}$

6. **Multi-Step Problem** The Fresh Fruit & Jelly Company sells three different gift arrangements consisting of various types of fruits and jellies. The basic arrangement of 2 fruits and 3 jelly jars costs $12. The large arrangement of 4 fruits and 5 jelly jars costs $21. The deluxe arrangement of 6 fruits and 10 jelly jars costs $40.

a. Write and solve a system of equations using the information about the basic and large arrangements.

b. Write and solve a system of equations using the information about the large and deluxe arrangements.

c. **Writing** Compare the results from parts (a) and (b) and make a statement about why there is a discrepancy.

NAME _____ DATE _____

Standardized Test Practice

For use with pages 249–255

TEST TAKING STRATEGY   **Try to find shortcuts that will help you move through the questions quicker.**

1. *Multiple Choice*   What is the vertex of the graph of $y = \frac{1}{4}(x - 2)^2 + 6$?

   (A) $(0, 7)$ (B) $(2, 6)$

   (C) $(-2, -6)$ (D) $(4, 7)$

   (E) $(-2, 6)$

2. *Multiple Choice*   What is the vertex of the graph of $y = -4(x - 1)(x + 5)$?

   (A) $(-2, -36)$ (B) $(1, -5)$

   (C) $(-1, 5)$ (D) $(-2, 36)$

   (E) $(-2, -9)$

3. *Multiple Choice*   What is the vertex of the graph of $y = 3x^2 - 12x + 13$?

   (A) $(-2, 1)$ (B) $(2, 1)$

   (C) $(-2, -1)$ (D) $(0, 13)$

   (E) $(2, -1)$

4. *Multiple Choice*   What is the axis of symmetry of the graph of $y = -\frac{1}{2}(x + 2)(x - 6)$?

   (A) $x = 6$ (B) $x = -2$

   (C) $x = 2$ (D) $x = -6$

   (E) $x = -12$

5. *Multi-Step Problem*   A golf ball is hit from ground level into the air following the path of the equation $y = -0.1x^2 + 10x$. (Assume the x-axis is at ground level.)

   a. If you assume the point at which the golf ball is hit is $(0, 0)$, at what point does the ball come down and hit the ground?

   b. If you assume x and y are measured in yards, how far was the ball from the golfer when it hit the ground?

   c. At what point did the golf ball reach its maximum height?

   d. What was the maximum height of the golf ball in terms of yards?

6. *Multiple Choice*   What is the standard form of the quadratic function

   $$y = -5(x + 2)^2 + 18?$$

   (A) $y = -5x^2 - 20x - 2$

   (B) $y = 5x^2 - 20x - 2$

   (C) $y = 5x^2 - 20x + 2$

   (D) $y = -5x^2 + 20x - 2$

   (E) $y = -5x^2 + 20x + 2$

Standardized Test Practice

For use with pages 256–263

TEST TAKING STRATEGY **If you get stuck on a question, select an answer choice and check to see if it is a reasonable answer to the question.**

1. *Multiple Choice* What is a correct factorization of $x^2 - 7x + 10$?

    Ⓐ $(x + 1)(x - 10)$ Ⓑ $(x + 2)(x - 5)$

    Ⓒ $(x - 2)(x - 5)$ Ⓓ $(x + 1)(x + 10)$

    Ⓔ $(x - 2)(x + 5)$

2. *Multiple Choice* What is a correct factorization of $x^2 + 6x - 16$?

    Ⓐ $(x + 8)(x - 2)$ Ⓑ $(x + 4)(x - 4)$

    Ⓒ $(x - 8)(x - 2)$ Ⓓ $(x - 4)(x - 4)$

    Ⓔ $(x - 8)(x + 2)$

3. *Multiple Choice* What is a correct factorization of $3x^2 - x - 4$?

    Ⓐ $(3x + 4)(x - 1)$ Ⓑ $(3x - 4)(x - 1)$

    Ⓒ $(3x - 1)(x + 4)$ Ⓓ $(3x + 4)(x + 1)$

    Ⓔ $(3x - 4)(x + 1)$

4. *Multiple Choice* If $x^2 - 6x + c$ is a perfect square trinomial, what is the value of c?

    Ⓐ 12   Ⓑ 9

    Ⓒ -12 Ⓓ 36

    Ⓔ -9

Quantitative Comparison **In Exercises 5–7, choose the statement below that is true about the given quantities.**

Ⓐ The number in column A is greater.

Ⓑ The number in column B is greater.

Ⓒ The two numbers are equal.

Ⓓ The relationship cannot be determined from the given information.

	Column A	Column B
5.	The value of a in the factorization of $x^2 - 8x + 15$; $(x - a)(x - 5)$	The value of b in the factorization of $x^2 - 8x + 15$; $(x - 3)(x - b)$
6.	The value of a in the factorization of $2x^2 + 11x - 6$; $(2x - 1)(x + a)$	The value of b in the factorization of $3x^2 - 16x - 12$; $(3x + 2)(x - b)$
7.	The value of a in the factorization of $6x^2 + x - 2$; $(ax - 1)(3x + 2)$	The value of b in the factorization of $3x^2 - 20x - 32$; $(x - b)(3x + 4)$

8. *Multiple Choice* What are all solutions of $2x^2 - 5x = x^2 - 6x + 2$?

    Ⓐ 1   Ⓑ 3

    Ⓒ -2 Ⓓ $-2, 1$

    Ⓔ 1, 3

Algebra 2
Standardized Test Practice Workbook

Standardized Test Practice

For use with pages 264–271

TEST TAKING STRATEGY   **During the test, do not worry excessively about how much time you have left. Concentrate on the question in front of you.**

1. *Multiple Choice*   What is the simplified form of the expression $\sqrt{162}$?

   Ⓐ $3\sqrt{18}$ Ⓑ $3\sqrt{54}$

   Ⓒ $9\sqrt{18}$ Ⓓ $\sqrt{3}\sqrt{54}$

   Ⓔ $9\sqrt{2}$

2. *Multiple Choice*   What is the simplified form of the expression $\sqrt{12} \cdot \sqrt{18}$?

   Ⓐ $\sqrt{216}$ Ⓑ $2\sqrt{54}$

   Ⓒ $6\sqrt{6}$ Ⓓ $3\sqrt{36}$

   Ⓔ $3\sqrt{24}$

3. *Multiple Choice*   What is the simplified form of the expression

   $$\sqrt{\frac{2}{15}}?$$

   Ⓐ $\dfrac{\sqrt{2}}{\sqrt{15}}$ Ⓑ $\dfrac{\sqrt{2}}{15}$

   Ⓒ $\dfrac{\sqrt{30}}{15}$ Ⓓ $\sqrt{2}$

   Ⓔ $\dfrac{2\sqrt{15}}{15}$

4. *Multiple Choice*   What are the solutions of $2x^2 - 3 = 13$?

   Ⓐ $\pm\sqrt{2}$ Ⓑ $\pm2\sqrt{2}$

   Ⓒ $2\sqrt{2}$ Ⓓ ±2

   Ⓔ $-\sqrt{2}$

Quantitative Comparison   **In Exercises 5–8, choose the statement below that is true about the given quantities.**

Ⓐ   The number in column A is greater.

Ⓑ   The number in column B is greater.

Ⓒ   The two numbers are equal.

Ⓓ   The relationship cannot be determined from the given information.

	Column A	Column B
5.	The value of x in $\sqrt{54} = 3\sqrt{x}$	The value of y in $\sqrt{108} = y\sqrt{3}$
6.	The value of x in $\dfrac{1}{2} = x^2$	The value of y in $\sqrt{\dfrac{4}{5}} = \dfrac{2\sqrt{5}}{y}$
7.	The solution(s) of $(x + 3)^2 = 0$	The solution(s) of $(x + 5)^2 = 0$
8.	The solution(s) of $\left(x - \dfrac{1}{2}\right)^2 = 0$	The solution(s) of $(x - 6)^2 = 0$

NAME _____ DATE _____

Standardized Test Practice

For use with pages 272–280

TEST TAKING STRATEGY **If you keep up your homework, both your problem-solving abilities and your vocabulary will improve.**

1. *Multiple Choice* What does the product $(-5 - 2i)(3 + 7i)$ equal?

   (A) $-15 - 14i^2$ (B) $-1 - 41i$

   (C) $-29 - 41i$ (D) $-1 + 41i$

   (E) $-29 + 41i$

2. *Multiple Choice* What does the product $(3 - 6i)(9 - 4i)$ equal?

   (A) $27 - 24i^2$ (B) $-51 - 66i$

   (C) $-3 + 66i$ (D) $3 - 42i$

   (E) $3 - 66i$

3. *Multiple Choice* What does the product $-3i(8 + 5i)$ equal?

   (A) $15 - 24i$ (B) $15i^2 - 24i$

   (C) $-15 + 24i$ (D) $-15 - 24i$

   (E) $15 + 24i$

4. *Multiple Choice* What does the quotient $\dfrac{3 + i}{2 + 3i}$ equal?

   (A) $\dfrac{3}{2} - \dfrac{1}{3}$ (B) $\dfrac{6 - 3i^2}{13}$

   (C) $\dfrac{9 - 7i}{13}$ (D) $\dfrac{3 - 7i}{-13}$

   (E) $\dfrac{-9 + 7i}{13}$

Quantitative Comparison   **In Exercises 5–7, choose the statement below that is true about the given quantities.**

   (A) The number in column A is greater.

   (B) The number in column B is greater.

   (C) The two numbers are equal.

   (D) The relationship cannot be determined from the given information.

	Column A	Column B
5.	$\lvert -3 + i \rvert$	$\lvert 1 - 3i \rvert$
6.	$\lvert 5i \rvert$	$\lvert -6 - i \rvert$
7.	$\lvert -4 + 3i \rvert$	$\lvert -5 + i \rvert$

8. *Multiple Choice* Which complex number is farthest from the origin in the complex plane?

   (A) $6i$ (B) $3 - 2i$

   (C) $6 + i$ (D) $-4 - 7i$

   (E) $-8i$

9. *Multiple Choice* Which complex number is farthest from the origin in the complex plane?

   (A) $-8 + i$ (B) $9 - i$

   (C) $4 + 2i$ (D) $-5 + 5i$

   (E) $9i$

Standardized Test Practice

For use with pages 281–290

TEST TAKING STRATEGY **When taking a test, first tackle the questions that you know are easy for you to answer.**

1. *Multiple Choice* If $x^2 + 10x + c$ is a perfect square trinomial, what is the value of c?

   (A) 5   (B) 10

   (C) 25   (D) 50

   (E) 100

2. *Multiple Choice* If $x^2 - 32x + c$ is a perfect square trinomial, what is the value of c?

   (A) 16   (B) 32

   (C) 96   (D) 256

   (E) 1024

3. *Multiple Choice* If $x^2 - x + c$ is a perfect square trinomial, what is the value of c?

   (A) $\dfrac{1}{8}$ (B) $\dfrac{1}{4}$

   (C) $\dfrac{1}{2}$ (D) 1

   (E) $\dfrac{3}{2}$

4. *Multiple Choice* What are the solutions of $x^2 + 5x - 7 = 0$?

   (A) $-5 \pm \sqrt{53}$ (B) $\dfrac{-5 \pm \sqrt{53}}{2}$

   (C) $\dfrac{5 \pm \sqrt{53}}{2}$ (D) $\dfrac{-5 - i\sqrt{53}}{2}$

   (E) $\dfrac{-5 + i\sqrt{53}}{2}$

Quantitative Comparison **In Exercises 5–7, choose the statement below that is true about the given quantities.**

   (A) The number in column A is greater.

   (B) The number in column B is greater.

   (C) The two numbers are equal.

   (D) The relationship cannot be determined from the given information.

	Column A	Column B
5.	The value of c that makes the expression $x^2 + 24x + c$ a perfect square trinomial	The value of c that makes the expression $x^2 - 14x + c$ a perfect square trinomial
6.	The value of a in the factorization of $2x^2 - 7x - 15$; $(ax + b)(x - 5)$	The value of b in the factorization of $6x^2 - 5x + 1$; $(cx - 1)(bx - 1)$
7.	The value of a in the solutions of $x^2 + 6x + 2 = 0$; $\left(-3 + \sqrt{a},\ -3 - \sqrt{a}\right)$	The value of b in the solutions of $x^2 - 10x - 3 = 0$; $\left(5 + 2\sqrt{b},\ 5 - 2\sqrt{b}\right)$

8. *Multiple Choice* What are the solutions of $x^2 - 3x + 9 = 0$?

   (A) $1 \pm \sqrt{3}$ (B) $\dfrac{-3 \pm 3i\sqrt{3}}{2}$

   (C) $\dfrac{-3 \pm i\sqrt{3}}{2}$ (D) $\dfrac{3 \pm 3i\sqrt{3}}{2}$

   (E) $\dfrac{3 \pm i\sqrt{3}}{2}$

Standardized Test Practice

For use with pages 291–298

TEST TAKING STRATEGY   **When taking a test, go back and answer questions that you suspect will take you extra time and effort.**

1. *Multiple Choice*   What are the solutions of $x^2 + x = 11$?

   (A) $\dfrac{1 + 3\sqrt{5}}{2}$ (B) $\dfrac{-1 \pm 3\sqrt{5}}{2}$

   (C) $\dfrac{-1 \pm 2\sqrt{3}}{2}$ (D) $\dfrac{1 \pm 3\sqrt{5}}{2}$

   (E) $\dfrac{1 \pm 2\sqrt{3}}{2}$

2. *Multiple Choice*   What are the solutions of $2x^2 + 9x + 2 = 0$?

   (A) $\dfrac{-9 \pm \sqrt{65}}{4}$ (B) $\dfrac{-9 + \sqrt{65}}{4}$

   (C) $\dfrac{-9 \pm 5\sqrt{13}}{4}$ (D) $\dfrac{-9 - 5\sqrt{13}}{4}$

   (E) $\dfrac{-9 - \sqrt{65}}{4}$

3. *Multiple Choice*   What are the solutions of $x^2 - 3x = -2x - 7$?

   (A) $\dfrac{1 \pm 3\sqrt{3}}{2}$ (B) $\dfrac{1 - 3i\sqrt{3}}{2}$

   (C) $\dfrac{1 \pm i\sqrt{6}}{2}$ (D) $\dfrac{1 + i\sqrt{6}}{2}$

   (E) $\dfrac{1 \pm 3i\sqrt{3}}{2}$

Quantitative Comparison   **In Exercises 4–7, choose the statement below that is true about the given quantities.**

   (A)   The number in column A is greater.

   (B)   The number in column B is greater.

   (C)   The two numbers are equal.

   (D)   The relationship cannot be determined from the given information.

	Column A	Column B
4.	Discriminant of $x^2 + 2x - 9 = 0$	Discriminant of $x^2 - 6x + 3 = 0$
5.	Discriminant of $2kx^2 + 2\sqrt{6}x - 2k = 0$	Discriminant of $2x^2 + 4kx - 3 = 0$
6.	Greatest zero of $f(x) = 5x^2 + 2x - 1$	Least zero of $f(x) = 3x^2 - 8x + 2$
7.	Least zero of $f(x) = 6x^2 + 7x - 4$	Greatest zero of $f(x) = 5x^2 - 12x - 14$

8. *Multiple Choice*   How many real and imaginary solutions does the equation $2x^2 - 7x + 9 = x + 1$ have?

   (A)   2 real solutions, no imaginary solutions

   (B)   1 real solution, no imaginary solutions

   (C)   1 real solution, 1 imaginary solution

   (D)   no real solutions, 2 imaginary solutions

   (E)   no real solutions, 1 imaginary solution

NAME _____ DATE _____

Standardized Test Practice

For use with pages 299–305

TEST TAKING STRATEGY   **During a test, draw graphs and figures in your test booklet to help you solve problems.**

1. *Multiple Choice*   What is the solution of $x^2 - 5x + 6 < 0$?

   Ⓐ $2 < x < 3$

   Ⓑ $x = 2$ or $x = 3$

   Ⓒ $x > -2$ or $x < 3$

   Ⓓ $x > 2$ or $x < 3$

   Ⓔ $-3 < x < 2$

2. *Multiple Choice*   What is the solution of $x^2 + x - 20 > 0$?

   Ⓐ $x = -5$ or $x = 4$

   Ⓑ $-5 < x < 4$

   Ⓒ $x > -5$ or $x < 4$

   Ⓓ $-4 < x < 5$

   Ⓔ $x < -5$ or $x > 4$

3. *Multiple Choice*   Which quadratic inequality is graphed?

   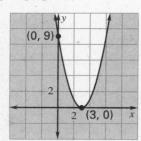

   Ⓐ $y \geq x^2 + 3$

   Ⓑ $y \leq x^2 + 3$

   Ⓒ $y \leq (x - 3)^2$

   Ⓓ $y \leq (x + 3)^2$

   Ⓔ $y \geq x^2 - 3$

4. *Multi-Step Problem*   A manufacturer has determined that the demand for a certain product is $q = -p^2 + 8p - 6$ and the supply equation for the same product is $q = p + 4$. The product's price per unit is p (in dollars) and q represents the number of units (in thousands).

   a. Graph both equations in the same coordinate plane.

   b. The points of intersection of the two graphs are called the points of equilibrium. What are the points of equilibrium for these two equations?

   c. What is the demand for the product at $4 per unit?

   d. What is the supply for the product at $5 per unit?

   e. *Critical Thinking*   Explain how the graph indicates that it does not make sense for the manufacturer to try to sell the product for more than $5.

5. *Multiple Choice*   Which quadratic inequality is graphed?

   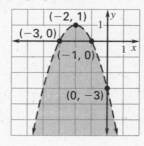

   Ⓐ $y < -x^2 - 4x - 3$

   Ⓑ $y < x^2 - 4x - 3$

   Ⓒ $y > x^2 - 4x - 3$

   Ⓓ $y > -x^2 - 4x - 3$

   Ⓔ $y > -x^2 + 4x - 3$

NAME _____ DATE _____

Standardized Test Practice

For use with pages 306–312

TEST TAKING STRATEGY   **Even though you must keep your answer sheet neat, you can make any kind of mark you want in your test booklet.**

1. *Multiple Choice*   Which quadratic function *cannot* be represented by the graph shown?

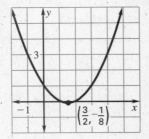

(A) $y = \frac{1}{2}(x + 2)(x + 1)$

(B) $y = \frac{1}{2}x^2 - \frac{3}{2}x + 1$

(C) $y = \frac{1}{2}\left(x - \frac{3}{2}\right)^2 - \frac{1}{8}$

(D) $y = \frac{1}{2}(x^2 - 3x + 2)$

(E) $y = \frac{1}{2}(x - 2)(x - 1)$

2. *Multiple Choice*   Which quadratic function *cannot* be represented by the graph shown?

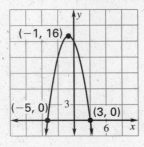

(A) $y = -(x - 3)(x + 5)$

(B) $y = -(x^2 + 2x - 15)$

(C) $y = -(x + 3)(x - 5)$

(D) $y = -x^2 - 2x + 15$

(E) $y = -(x + 1)^2 + 16$

3. *Multiple Choice*   Which quadratic function in vertex form has a graph with the vertex $(-2, -2)$ and passes through the point $(-3, 1)$?

(A) $y = -3(x + 2)^2 + 2$

(B) $y = 3(x - 2)^2 - 2$

(C) $y = 3(x + 2)^2 + 2$

(D) $y = 3(x + 2)^2 - 2$

(E) $y = 3(x - 2)^2 + 2$

4. *Multiple Choice*   Which quadratic function in vertex form has a graph with the vertex $(-3, -6)$ and passes through the point $(2, -31)$?

(A) $y = -(x + 3)^2 + 6$

(B) $y = (x + 3)^2 - 6$

(C) $y = -(x + 3)^2 - 6$

(D) $y = -(x - 3)^2 - 6$

(E) $y = (x + 3)^2 + 6$

5. *Multi-Step Problem*   The table below shows the number of phone calls p that a salesperson makes and the actual number of face-to-face appointments a with potential customers arranged by those phone calls.

Appointments, *a*	8	10	11	14	15	18
Phone calls, *p*	22	34	42	66	78	110

a. Find the ratios $\frac{p}{a}$. Do phone calls vary directly with appointments?

b. Find the ratios $\frac{p}{a^2}$. What do you notice?

c. Use the result of part (b) to write a quadratic model for p as a function of a.

d. Find the number of phone calls required if the salesperson needs to arrange 25 appointments.

TEST TAKING STRATEGY **Long-term preparation for a standardized test can be done through-out your high school career and can improve your overall abilities.**

1. *Multiple Choice* What is the value of $-2^2 \cdot 2^4$?

(A) -64 (B) 64

(C) -256 (D) 256

(E) -4096

2. *Multiple Choice* What is the value of $(3^2)^3$?

(A) 27 (B) 54

(C) 216 (D) 243

(E) 729

3. *Multiple Choice* What is the simplified form of $(-5x^{-2})^3 x^7$?

(A) $-5x$ (B) $25x$

(C) $-125x^8$ (D) $-125x$

(E) $125x^8$

4. *Multiple Choice* What is the simplified form of

$$\left(\frac{2x^{-3}}{3y^{-4}}\right)^{-2}?$$

(A) $\dfrac{2x^6}{3y^8}$ (B) $\dfrac{3y^8}{2x^6}$

(C) $\dfrac{9y^6}{4x^5}$ (D) $\dfrac{9y^8}{4x^6}$

(E) $\dfrac{9x^6}{4y^8}$

Quantitative Comparison **In Exercises 5–8, choose the statement below that is true about the given quantities.**

(A) The number in column A is greater.

(B) The number in column B is greater.

(C) The two numbers are equal.

(D) The relationship cannot be determined from the given information.

	Column A	Column B
5.	$(4^0)(6^2)$	$(-3)^2(2^2)$
6.	$(-5)^{-2}(4)^{-1}$	10^{-2}
7.	$\left(\dfrac{2}{7}\right)^{-3}$	$\left(\dfrac{4}{5}\right)^{-3}$
8.	3.6×10^{-11}	1.2×10^{-10}

9. *Multiple Choice* What is 1.25×10^{-4} divided by 2.50×10^8?

(A) 0.50×10^{12} (B) 0.50×10^{-13}

(C) 5.0×10^{-13} (D) 5.0×10^{-12}

(E) 5.0×10^{12}

Standardized Test Practice

TEST TAKING STRATEGY   **Do not panic if you run out of time before answering all of the questions. You can still receive a high score on a standardized test without answering every question.**

1. *Multiple Choice*   Which one of the following is a polynomial function?

   Ⓐ $f(x) = 2x^2 - 4^x$

   Ⓑ $f(x) = 3x^3 - 2x^{-2} + x$

   Ⓒ $f(x) = -5x^{-4} - 3^{x-2}$

   Ⓓ $f(x) = x^2 + \sqrt{3}x - 7$

   Ⓔ $f(x) = 2^x + 9x$

2. *Multiple Choice*   What type of polynomial function is $f(x) = 4x^3 - 2x^2 - x + 11$?

   Ⓐ constant   Ⓑ linear

   Ⓒ quadratic   Ⓓ cubic

   Ⓔ quartic

3. *Multiple Choice*   What is the value of $f(x) = 6x^4 - 3x^3 + 5x^2 - x + 6$ when $x = 2$?

   Ⓐ 88   Ⓑ 96

   Ⓒ −96   Ⓓ 148

   Ⓔ −148

4. *Multiple Choice*   What is the value of $f(x) = -8x^5 + 6x^4 - 5x^3 + 10x^2 + 9x - 1$ when $x = -1$?

   Ⓐ 11   Ⓑ −9

   Ⓒ 7   Ⓓ −11

   Ⓔ 19

5. *Multi-Step Problem*   To determine whether a Holstein heifer's height is normal, a veterinarian can use the cubic functions

   $$L = 0.0007t^3 - 0.061t^2 + 2.02t + 30$$

   $$H = 0.001t^3 - 0.08t^2 + 2.3t + 31$$

   where L is the minimum normal height (in inches), H is the maximum normal height (in inches), and t is the age (in months).

   a. What is the normal height range for a 12-month-old Holstein heifer?

   b. Describe the end behavior of each function's graph.

   c. Graph the two height functions.

   d. *Writing*   Suppose a veterinarian examines a Holstein heifer that is 36 inches tall. How old do you think the heifer is? How did you get your answer?

6. *Multiple Choice*   What is the time t (in seconds) it takes a camera battery to recharge after 150 flashes if the recharge time can be modeled by $t = 0.000015n^3 - 0.0034n^2 + 0.25n + 5.3$ where n is the number of flashes?

   Ⓐ about 17 seconds

   Ⓑ about 20 seconds

   Ⓒ about 21 seconds

   Ⓓ about 24 seconds

   Ⓔ about 25 seconds

Algebra 2
Standardized Test Practice Workbook

Standardized Test Practice

For use with pages 338–344

TEST TAKING STRATEGY   **Long-term preparation will definitely affect not only your standardized test scores, but your overall future academic performance as well.**

1. **Multiple Choice**   What is the sum of $7x^3 + 6x^2 - 5x + 5$ and $-6x^3 - 8x^2 + 10x - 7$?

   Ⓐ $x^3 + 2x^2 + 5x + 2$

   Ⓑ $x^3 - 2x^2 + 5x - 2$

   Ⓒ $-x^3 - 2x^2 + 5x - 2$

   Ⓓ $x^3 - 2x^2 - 5x + 2$

   Ⓔ $x^3 + 2x^2 - 5x - 2$

2. **Multiple Choice**   What is $5x^3 - 2x^2 + 9x - 3$ subtracted from $9x^3 - 18x^2 - 6x + 4$?

   Ⓐ $14x^3 - 20x^2 + 3x + 1$

   Ⓑ $-4x^3 + 16x^2 + 15x - 7$

   Ⓒ $4x^3 + 16x^2 + 3x + 7$

   Ⓓ $4x^3 - 16x^2 + 15x + 1$

   Ⓔ $4x^3 - 16x^2 - 15x + 7$

3. **Multiple Choice**   What is the product of $(-2x^2 + 3x - 1)$ and $(x - 2)$?

   Ⓐ $-2x^3 - 6x + 2$

   Ⓑ $2x^3 - 7x^2 + 7x - 2$

   Ⓒ $-2x^3 + 7x^2 - 7x + 2$

   Ⓓ $-2x^3 + 7x^2 + 7x + 2$

   Ⓔ $-2x^3 - 7x^2 + 7x - 2$

4. **Multiple Choice**   What does $(x + 5)(x - 2)(x + 1)$ equal?

   Ⓐ $x^3 - 4x^2 - 7x - 10$

   Ⓑ $x^3 + 4x^2 - 7x - 10$

   Ⓒ $x^3 + 4x^2 + 7x + 10$

   Ⓓ $x^3 + 4x^2 + 7x - 10$

   Ⓔ $x^3 - 4x^2 - 7x + 10$

5. **Multiple Choice** $(2x - 5)^3 = $ ___?___

   Ⓐ $8x^3 - 30x^2 + 150x - 125$

   Ⓑ $8x^3 - 60x^2 - 150x - 125$

   Ⓒ $8x^3 + 60x^2 - 150x + 125$

   Ⓓ $8x^3 - 60x^2 + 150x - 125$

   Ⓔ $8x^3 - 60x^2 + 150x + 125$

6. **Multi-Step Problem**   Suppose two sisters each make three deposits in accounts earning the same annual interest rate r (expressed as a decimal).

Simmons, Marta

Date	Transaction	Amount
1/1/98	Deposit	$2000.00
1/1/99	Deposit	$3600.00
1/1/00	Deposit	$3200.00

Simmons, Lauren

Date	Transaction	Amount
1/1/98	Deposit	$2500.00
1/1/99	Deposit	$3000.00
1/1/00	Deposit	$4600.00

a. Write the worth of Marta's account on January 1, 2001 as a sum of expressions in the form $P(1 + r)^t$ where P is the amount deposited, r is the rate (expressed as a decimal), and t is the number of years. Write a similar sum for the worth of Lauren's account on January 1, 2001.

b. Find the total value of the two accounts and write it as a polynomial in standard form.

c. **Writing**   Explain how to find the total worth of both accounts on January 1, 2001 if the rate is a constant 6% over the three years.

Chapter 6

TEST TAKING STRATEGY **The mathematical portion of a standardized test is based on concepts and skills taught in high school mathematics courses.**

1. *Multiple Choice* Which of the following is the factorization of $x^3 + 64$?

Ⓐ $(x + 4)(x^2 + 4x + 16)$
Ⓑ $(x - 4)(x^2 - 4x - 16)$
Ⓒ $(x - 4)(x^2 - 4x + 16)$
Ⓓ $(x + 4)(x^2 + 4x - 16)$
Ⓔ $(x + 4)(x^2 - 4x + 16)$

2. *Multiple Choice* Which of the following is the factorization of $8x^3 - 125$?

Ⓐ $(2x - 5)(4x^2 + 10x + 25)$
Ⓑ $(2x - 5)(4x^2 - 10x + 25)$
Ⓒ $(2x + 5)(4x^2 - 10x - 25)$
Ⓓ $(2x + 5)(4x^2 + 10x - 25)$
Ⓔ $(2x - 5)(4x^2 - 10x - 25)$

3. *Multiple Choice* Which polynomial has the factorization $(4x - 3)(16x^2 + 12x + 9)$?

Ⓐ $64x^3 - 27$ Ⓑ $64x^3 + 27$
Ⓒ $64x^3 - 48$ Ⓓ $64x^3 - 27x^2$
Ⓔ $64x^3 - 48x^2$

4. *Multiple Choice* What are all the *real* solutions of the equation $x^3 - 13x = 12$?

Ⓐ $-3, 1$ Ⓑ $-3, -1, 4$
Ⓒ $-3, 1, 4$ Ⓓ $-1, 4$
Ⓔ 4

Quantitative Comparison **In Exercises 5–7, choose the statement below that is true about the given quantities.**

Ⓐ The number in column A is greater.
Ⓑ The number in column B is greater.
Ⓒ The two numbers are equal.
Ⓓ The relationship cannot be determined from the given information.

	Column A	Column B
5.	The coefficient a in the factorization of $27x^3 - 8$; $(3x - 2)(ax^2 + bx + c)$	The coefficient b in the factorization of $27x^3 - 8$; $(3x - 2)(ax^2 + bx + c)$
6.	The constant a in the factorization of $x^3 - 4x^2 - 25x + 100$; $(x - 4)(x + a)(x - b)$	The constant b in the factorization of $x^3 - 4x^2 - 25x + 100$; $(x - 4)(x + a)(x - b)$
7.	The greatest solution of $x^3 + 12x^2 + 48x + 64 = 0$	The least solution of $x^3 - 2x^2 - 19x + 20 = 0$

8. *Multiple Choice* Which of the following is the factorization of $x^3 - 5x^2 - 16x + 80$?

Ⓐ $(x - 4)(x + 4)(x + 5)$
Ⓑ $(x - 4)^2(x + 5)$
Ⓒ $(x - 4)(x + 5)^2$
Ⓓ $(x - 4)(x + 4)(x - 5)$
Ⓔ $(x + 4)^2(x + 5)$

NAME _____ DATE _____

Standardized Test Practice

For use with pages 352–358

TEST TAKING STRATEGY **Even though you must keep your answer sheet neat, you can make any kind of mark you want in your test booklet.**

1. *Multiple Choice*   What is the result of dividing $x^3 - 6x + 7$ by $x - 2$?

Ⓐ $x^2 - 2x - 2 + \dfrac{11}{x - 2}$

Ⓑ $x^2 - 2x - 2 + \dfrac{3}{x - 2}$

Ⓒ $x^2 + 2x - 2 + \dfrac{3}{x - 2}$

Ⓓ $x^2 + 2x - 2 - \dfrac{11}{x - 2}$

Ⓔ $x^2 - 2x + 2 + \dfrac{3}{x - 2}$

2. *Multiple Choice*   What is the result of dividing $3x^3 + 7x^2 + 5$ by $x + 1$?

Ⓐ $3x^2 + 10x + 10 + \dfrac{15}{x + 1}$

Ⓑ $3x^2 + 4x + 4 + \dfrac{1}{x + 1}$

Ⓒ $3x^2 - 10x + 10 - \dfrac{15}{x + 1}$

Ⓓ $3x^2 - 4x - 4 + \dfrac{9}{x + 1}$

Ⓔ $3x^2 + 4x - 4 + \dfrac{9}{x + 1}$

3. *Multiple Choice*   What is the factorization of $f(x) = 2x^3 - x^2 - 5x - 2$ given that $f(2) = 0$?

Ⓐ $(x - 2)(2x + 1)(x + 1)$

Ⓑ $(x - 2)(2x - 1)(x + 1)$

Ⓒ $(x - 2)(2x + 1)(x - 1)$

Ⓓ $(x - 2)(2x - 1)(x - 1)$

Ⓔ $(x + 2)(2x + 1)(x - 1)$

4. *Multiple Choice*   What are the other zeros of $f(x) = 3x^3 + 17x^2 + 18x - 8$ if one zero is $x = -4$?

Ⓐ $\dfrac{1}{3}, 2$ Ⓑ $-\dfrac{1}{3}, 2$

Ⓒ $-1, \dfrac{2}{3}$ Ⓓ $\dfrac{1}{3}, -2$

Ⓔ $-\dfrac{2}{3}, 1$

Quantitative Comparison   **In Exercises 5 and 6, choose the statement below that is true about the given quantities.**

Ⓐ   The number in column A is greater.

Ⓑ   The number in column B is greater.

Ⓒ   The two numbers are equal.

Ⓓ   The relationship cannot be determined from the given information.

	Column A	Column B
5.	The greatest remaining zero of the function $f(x) =$ $x^3 + 8x^2 + 11x - 20$ if one zero is $x = -4$	The least remaining zero of the function $f(x) =$ $x^3 - 9x^2 + 26x - 24$ if one zero is $x = 4$
6.	The greatest remaining zero of the function $f(x) =$ $x^3 - 3x^2 - 4x + 12$ if one zero is $x = -2$	The least remaining zero of the function $f(x) =$ $x^3 - 3x^2 - 16x + 48$ if one zero is $x = -4$

7. *Multiple Choice*   Which of the following is a factor of the polynomial $2x^3 + 5x^2 - 4x - 3$?

Ⓐ $2x + 1$ Ⓑ $x + 1$

Ⓒ $x - 3$ Ⓓ $2x - 1$

Ⓔ $2x - 3$

Standardized Test Practice

For use with pages 359–365

TEST TAKING STRATEGY   **If you get stuck on a question, select an answer choice and check to see if it is a reasonable answer to the question.**

1. *Multiple Choice*   What are all the rational zeros of $f(x) = x^3 - x^2 - 17x - 15$?

   Ⓐ $-3, -1, 5$ Ⓑ $-3, 1, 5$

   Ⓒ $-5, -1, 3$ Ⓓ $-5, 1, 3$

   Ⓔ $-1, 3, 5$

2. *Multiple Choice*   What are all the rational zeros of $f(x) = x^3 - 3x^2 - 40x + 84$?

   Ⓐ $-7, -6, -2$ Ⓑ $-6, -2, 7$

   Ⓒ $-6, 2, 7$ Ⓓ $-2, 6, 7$

   Ⓔ $2, 6, 7$

3. *Multiple Choice*   What are all the real zeros of $f(x) = x^4 - 5x^2 + 4$?

   Ⓐ $1, 2$ Ⓑ $\pm 1, 2$

   Ⓒ $-1, 2$ Ⓓ $-1, \pm 2$

   Ⓔ $\pm 1, \pm 2$

4. *Multiple Choice*   What are all the real zeros of $f(x) = 2x^3 - 11x^2 + 8x - 15$?

   Ⓐ $-1, -5$ Ⓑ $-1, 5$

   Ⓒ 5 Ⓓ 1

   Ⓔ -5

5. *Multiple Choice*   What are all the real zeros of $f(x) = x^4 - 2x^3 - 23x^2 + 24x + 144$?

   Ⓐ $-3, 4$ Ⓑ $\pm 3, 4$

   Ⓒ $-4, 3$ Ⓓ $-4, \pm 3$

   Ⓔ $\pm 3, \pm 4$

Quantitative Comparison   **In Exercises 6–9, choose the statement below that is true about the given quantities.**

   Ⓐ   The number in column A is greater.

   Ⓑ   The number in column B is greater.

   Ⓒ   The two numbers are equal.

   Ⓓ   The relationship cannot be determined from the given information.

	Column A	Column B
6.	The number of possible rational zeros of $f(x) = x^4 - 3x^3 + 2x^2 + 18$	The number of possible rational zeros of $f(x) = x^3 - 2x^2 + 6x + 24$
7.	The number of possible rational zeros of $f(x) = x^3 + 5x^2 - 7x + 6$	The number of possible rational zeros of $f(x) = x^4 - 10x^3 + 5x^2 - x - 10$
8.	The greatest real zero of $f(x) = x^3 - 4x^2 - 14x + 12$	The greatest real zero of $f(x) = x^3 - 12x^2 + 20x - 48$
9.	The greatest real zero of $f(x) = x^3 + 9x^2 + 26x + 24$	The greatest real zero of $f(x) = x^3 + 12x^2 + 47x + 60$

10. *Multiple Choice*   What are all the real zeros of $f(x) = x^4 + 2x^3 + x^2 - 4$?

   Ⓐ $-2, -1$ Ⓑ $-2, 1$

   Ⓒ $-1, 2$ Ⓓ $1, 2$

   Ⓔ $\pm 1, \pm 2$

TEST TAKING STRATEGY **When checking your answer to a question, try using a method different from one you used to get the answer.**

1. *Multiple Choice* How many zeros does the function $f(x) = 2x^5 - 3x^3 + x$ have?

   Ⓐ 1   Ⓑ 2

   Ⓒ 3   Ⓓ 4

   Ⓔ 5

2. *Multiple Choice* How many zeros does the function $f(x) = -3x^4 + 2x^3 + 7x - 5$ have?

   Ⓐ 1   Ⓑ 2

   Ⓒ 3   Ⓓ 4

   Ⓔ 5

3. *Multiple Choice* What are the zeros of $f(x) = x^3 - 11x^2 + 39x - 45$?

   Ⓐ $\pm 3, 5$ Ⓑ $3, 5$

   Ⓒ $-3, 5$ Ⓓ $-5, 3$

   Ⓔ $\pm 3i, 5$

4. *Multiple Choice* What are the zeros of $f(x) = x^3 - 2x^2 + x - 2$?

   Ⓐ 2 Ⓑ $1, 2$

   Ⓒ $i, \pm 2$ Ⓓ $\pm i, 2$

   Ⓔ $\pm 1, 2$

Quantitative Comparison **In Exercises 5 and 6, choose the statement below that is true about the given quantities.**

   Ⓐ The number in column A is greater.

   Ⓑ The number in column B is greater.

   Ⓒ The two numbers are equal.

   Ⓓ The relationship cannot be determined from the given information.

	Column A	Column B
5.	Number of zeros of the function $f(x) = -6x^3 - 2x^2 + 8$	Number of zeros of the function $f(x) = x^5 + 4x^2 + 3$
6.	Number of zeros of the function $f(x) = x^3 - 5x^4$	Number of zeros of the function $f(x) = x^4 + 7x^2$

7. *Multiple Choice* What is the polynomial function of least degree that has real coefficients, a leading coefficient of 1, and the zeros -1, 3, and 4?

   Ⓐ $f(x) = x^3 - 6x^2 + 5x + 12$

   Ⓑ $f(x) = x^3 - 6x^2 - 5x + 12$

   Ⓒ $f(x) = x^3 - 6x^2 - 5x - 12$

   Ⓓ $f(x) = x^3 - 6x^2 + 5x - 12$

   Ⓔ $f(x) = x^3 + 6x^2 - 5x - 12$

8. *Multiple Choice* What is the polynomial function of least degree that has real coefficients, a leading coefficient of 1, and the zeros $1, 2$, and $\pm 2i$?

   Ⓐ $f(x) = x^4 + 3x^3 - 6x^2 + 12x - 8$

   Ⓑ $f(x) = x^4 - 3x^3 - 6x^2 - 12x - 8$

   Ⓒ $f(x) = x^4 - 3x^3 + 6x^2 - 12x + 8$

   Ⓓ $f(x) = x^4 - 3x^3 + 6x^2 - 12x - 8$

   Ⓔ $f(x) = x^4 - 3x^3 + 6x^2 + 12x + 8$

Standardized Test Practice

For use with pages 373–378

TEST TAKING STRATEGY **If the answer to a question is formulas, substitute the given numbers into the formulas to test the possible answers.**

1. *Multiple Choice* Which graph of the function has the end behavior $f(x) \to -\infty$ as $x \to -\infty$ and $f(x) \to +\infty$ as $x \to +\infty$?

Ⓐ $f(x) = \frac{1}{3}(x + 6)(x - 5)^2$

Ⓑ $f(x) = -(x + 8)(x - 2)^2$

Ⓒ $f(x) = \frac{1}{4}(-x + 1)(x + 3)^2$

Ⓓ $f(x) = 5(x - 9)^2(x - 4)^2$

Ⓔ $f(x) = (-2x - 5)^2(x + 6)^2$

2. *Multiple Choice* Which graph of the function has the end behavior $f(x) \to -\infty$ as $x \to +\infty$ and $f(x) \to +\infty$ as $x \to -\infty$?

Ⓐ $f(x) = 4(x - 9)(x + 3)^2$

Ⓑ $f(x) = -\frac{3}{4}(x - 1)^2(x - 8)^2$

Ⓒ $f(x) = \frac{2}{3}(x + 1)(-x - 8)^2$

Ⓓ $f(x) = -(x + 3)(x - 11)^2$

Ⓔ $f(x) = (-x - 3)^2(-x + 10)^2$

3. *Multiple Choice* What is the local minimum of $f(x) = x^3 - 6x^2 + 10$?

Ⓐ $(1, 5)$ Ⓑ $(0, 10)$

Ⓒ $(2, -6)$ Ⓓ $(-2, 12)$

Ⓔ $(4, -22)$

4. *Multiple Choice* What is the local maximum of $f(x) = -2x^3 + 3x^2 - 4$?

Ⓐ $(0, -4)$ Ⓑ $(1, -3)$

Ⓒ $(2, 24)$ Ⓓ $(-1, 1)$

Ⓔ $(-2, 24)$

5. *Multi-Step Problem* You are designing a monument for the city park. The monument is to be a rectangular prism with dimensions $x + 2$ feet, $x - 1$ feet, and $x - 5$ feet.

a. Write a function $f(x)$ for the volume of the monument.

b. Use a graphing calculator to graph $f(x)$ for $-10 \le x \le 10$.

c. *Writing* Look back at your graph from part (b). Identify the local maximums and local minimums. Do these values represent maximum and minimum possible volumes of the monument? Explain.

d. If the volume of the monument is to be 210 cubic feet, what will the dimensions be?

6. Which function is graphed?

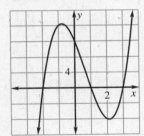

Ⓐ $f(x) = \frac{1}{2}(x - 1)(x + 2)(x - 3)$

Ⓑ $f(x) = -\frac{1}{2}(x - 1)(x + 2)(x - 3)$

Ⓒ $f(x) = 2(x - 1)(x + 2)(x - 3)$

Ⓓ $f(x) = (x - 1)(x - 2)(x + 3)$

Ⓔ $f(x) = -2(x + 1)(x - 2)(x + 3)$

Standardized Test Practice

For use with pages 380–386

TEST TAKING STRATEGY   **If you find yourself spending too much time on one question and getting frustrated, move on to the next question.**

1. **Multiple Choice**   Which cubic function is graphed?

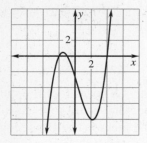

Ⓐ $f(x) = \frac{1}{3}(x - 1)(x + 2)(x - 4)$

Ⓑ $f(x) = -\frac{1}{3}(x + 1)(x + 2)(x + 4)$

Ⓒ $f(x) = \frac{1}{3}(x + 1)(x + 2)(x - 4)$

Ⓓ $f(x) = 3(x - 1)(x - 2)(x + 4)$

Ⓔ $f(x) = \frac{1}{3}(x + 1)(x + 2)(x + 4)$

2. **Multiple Choice**   The graph of which cubic function passes through the points $(3, 0)$, $(-4, 0)$, $(2, 0)$, and $(1, 5)$?

Ⓐ $f(x) = 2(x - 3)(x + 4)(x - 2)$

Ⓑ $f(x) = \frac{1}{2}(x - 3)(x + 4)(x - 2)$

Ⓒ $f(x) = -\frac{1}{2}(x - 3)(x + 4)(x - 2)$

Ⓓ $f(x) = -2(x - 3)(x + 4)(x - 2)$

Ⓔ $f(x) = (x - 3)(x + 4)(x - 2)$

3. **Multiple Choice**   Which cubic function models the data shown?

x	1	2	3	4	5
$f(x)$	-3	16	57	126	229

Ⓐ $f(x) = x^3 + 5x^2 + 3x - 6$

Ⓑ $f(x) = -x^3 + 5x^2 - 3x + 6$

Ⓒ $f(x) = x^3 - 5x^2 + 3x - 6$

Ⓓ $f(x) = -x^3 - 5x^2 - 3x - 6$

Ⓔ $f(x) = x^3 + 5x^2 - 3x - 6$

4. **Multi-Step Problem**   Your friend has a house-cleaning service and your cousin has a lawn-care service. You plan to start a small business of your own. You are trying to decide which of the two services you should choose. The profits for the first 6 months are shown in the table.

House-cleaning service	Month, t	1	2	3	4	5	6
	Profit, P	4	10	33	73	130	204
Lawn-care service	Month, t	1	2	3	4	5	6
	Profit, P	4	12	36	76	132	204

a. Use finite differences to find a polynomial model for each business.

b. **Writing**   You want to choose the business that will make the greater profit in December (when $t = 12$). Explain which business you should choose and why.

Standardized Test Practice

TEST TAKING STRATEGY   **When taking a test, first tackle the questions that you know are easy for you to answer.**

1. *Multiple Choice*   What is the value of $-64^{1/3}$?

   Ⓐ 4

   Ⓑ -4

   Ⓒ $\dfrac{1}{4}$

   Ⓓ $-\dfrac{1}{4}$

   Ⓔ $\pm\dfrac{1}{4}$

2. *Multiple Choice*   What is the value of $4^{5/2}$?

   Ⓐ 10

   Ⓑ -32

   Ⓒ $\dfrac{1}{32}$

   Ⓓ $\dfrac{1}{10}$

   Ⓔ 32

3. *Multiple Choice*   What is the value of $25^{-3/2}$?

   Ⓐ ± 125

   Ⓑ $\dfrac{1}{125}$

   Ⓒ 125

   Ⓓ $-\dfrac{1}{125}$

   Ⓔ $\pm\dfrac{1}{125}$

4. *Multiple Choice*   What is the value of $\left(\dfrac{1}{243}\right)^{-2/5}$?

   Ⓐ 9

   Ⓑ ± 9

   Ⓒ $\dfrac{1}{9}$

   Ⓓ -9

   Ⓔ $\pm\dfrac{1}{9}$

5. *Multiple Choice*   If $x^6 = 64$, what does x equal?

   Ⓐ 2

   Ⓑ -2

   Ⓒ ± 2

   Ⓓ ± 4

   Ⓔ 4

6. *Multiple Choice*   If $3x^5 = -729$, what does x equal?

   Ⓐ 3

   Ⓑ ± 3

   Ⓒ -3

   Ⓓ 9

   Ⓔ ± 9

7. *Multi-Step Problem*   A board foot is a unit for measuring wood. One board foot has a volume of 144 cubic inches. The Doyle log rule, given by

$$b = l\left(\dfrac{r-2}{2}\right)^2,$$

is a formula for approximating the number b of board feet in a log with length l (in feet) and radius r (in inches). The total volume V (in cubic inches) of wood in the main trunk of a Douglas fir can be modeled by $V = 250r^3$ where r is the radius of the trunk at the base of the tree. Suppose you need 6000 board feet from a 40 foot Douglas fir log.

   a. What volume of wood do you need?

   b. What is the radius of a log that will meet your needs?

   c. What is the total volume of wood in the main trunk of a Douglas fir that will meet your needs?

   d. If you find a suitable tree, what fraction of the tree would you actually use?

   e. *Writing*   How does your answer in part (d) change if you instead need only 2000 board feet?

NAME _____ DATE _____

Standardized Test Practice

For use with pages 407–414

TEST TAKING STRATEGY   **If you start to get tense during a test, put your pencil down and take some deep breaths. This may help you regain control.**

1. *Multiple Choice*   What is $6^{1/2} \cdot 6^{1/4}$?

   (A) $6^{1/8}$ (B) $36^{1/8}$

   (C) $36^{1/6}$ (D) $6^{1/6}$

   (E) $6^{3/4}$

2. *Multiple Choice*   What is $\sqrt[5]{4} \cdot \sqrt[5]{8}$?

   (A) -2 (B) 2

   (C) -3 (D) 3

   (E) 4

3. *Multiple Choice*   What is the simplified form of $\sqrt[4]{162}$?

   (A) $3\sqrt{2}$ (B) $3\sqrt[3]{2}$

   (C) $3\sqrt[4]{2}$ (D) $2\sqrt[3]{3}$

   (E) $2\sqrt[4]{3}$

4. *Multiple Choice*   What is $3(5^{1/3}) + 4(5^{1/3})$?

   (A) $35^{1/3}$ (B) $7^{1/3}$

   (C) $7(5^{1/3})$ (D) $12(5^{1/3})$

   (E) $7(25^{1/3})$

Quantitative Comparison   **In Exercises 5–7, choose the statement below that is true about the given quantities.**

   (A) The number in column A is greater.

   (B) The number in column B is greater.

   (C) The two numbers are equal.

   (D) The relationship cannot be determined from the given information.

	Column A	Column B
5.	$8^{1/3}$	$32^{1/5}$
6.	$-27^{2/3}$	$\left(\frac{1}{100}\right)^{-1/2}$
7.	$\sqrt[3]{6} \cdot \sqrt[3]{12}$	$\sqrt{3} \cdot \sqrt{24}$

8. *Multiple Choice*   What is the simplified form of

   $$\sqrt[5]{\frac{x^5}{y^{15}}}?$$

   (A) $\dfrac{x}{y^3}$ (B) $\dfrac{x^5}{y^{15}}$

   (C) $\dfrac{x^3}{y^5}$ (D) $\sqrt[5]{\dfrac{x}{y^3}}$

   (E) $\dfrac{x}{\sqrt[5]{y^3}}$

Standardized Test Practice

For use with pages 415–420

TEST TAKING STRATEGY   **During a test it is important to stay mentally focused, but also physically relaxed.**

1. *Multiple Choice*   Which of the following is true if $f(x) = 3x^{1/2}$, $g(x) = 2x^{-1/4}$ and $h(x) = 6x^{1/4}$?

   Ⓐ $h(x) = f(x) + g(x)$

   Ⓑ $h(x) = f(x) - g(x)$

   Ⓒ $h(x) = f(x) \cdot g(x)$

   Ⓓ $h(x) = \dfrac{f(x)}{g(x)}$

   Ⓔ $h(x) = f(g(x))$

2. *Multiple Choice*   Which of the following is true if $f(x) = 10x^{5/4}$, $g(x) = -2x^{3/8}$ and $h(x) = -5x^{7/8}$?

   Ⓐ $h(x) = f(x) + g(x)$

   Ⓑ $h(x) = f(x) - g(x)$

   Ⓒ $h(x) = f(x) \cdot g(x)$

   Ⓓ $h(x) = \dfrac{f(x)}{g(x)}$

   Ⓔ $h(x) = f(g(x))$

3. *Multiple Choice*   If $f(x) = x^2 + x - 1$ and $g(x) = x + 3$, what is $f(g(x))$?

   Ⓐ $x^2 + x + 2$ Ⓑ $x^2 + x + 8$

   Ⓒ $x^2 - 7x + 11$ Ⓓ $x^2 + 7x + 11$

   Ⓔ $x^2 + x - 2$

4. *Multiple Choice*   If $f(x) = 3x - 4$ and $g(x) = x^2 + 1$, what is $g(f(x))$?

   Ⓐ $9x^2 - 24x + 17$ Ⓑ $9x^2 - 12x + 17$

   Ⓒ $3x^2 - 1$ Ⓓ $3x^2 - 3$

   Ⓔ $9x^2 - 24x + 16$

5. A shoe store advertises that it is having a 20% off sale. For one day only, the store advertises an additional savings of 10%. What would be the sale price of a $50 pair of shoes?

   Ⓐ $15   Ⓑ $26

   Ⓒ $35   Ⓓ $36

   Ⓔ $42

Quantitative Comparison   **In Exercises 6–8, choose the statement below that is true about the given quantities.**

Ⓐ   The number in column A is greater.

Ⓑ   The number in column B is greater.

Ⓒ   The two numbers are equal.

Ⓓ   The relationship cannot be determined from the given information.

	Column A	Column B
6.	$f(g(3))$ where $f(x) = -2x$ and $g(x) = 7x^2$	$f(g(1))$ where $f(x) = x^{1/2}$ and $g(x) = 4x$
7.	$g(g(0))$ where $f(x) = x^2$ and $g(x) = x^2 + 3$	$f(f(-2))$ where $f(x) = -4x^2$ and $g(x) = x^4$
8.	$f(g(2))$ where $f(x) = \sqrt{x}$ and $g(x) = 6x^3$	$g(f(9))$ where $f(x) = x^{1/2}$ and $g(x) = 4\sqrt{x}$

TEST TAKING STRATEGY **You can always return to a more difficult problem later with a fresh perspective.**

1. *Multiple Choice* Which function is the inverse of $f(x) = -\frac{1}{5}x + 8$?

Ⓐ $f^{-1}(x) = \frac{1}{5}x + 8$

Ⓑ $f^{-1}(x) = -\frac{1}{5}x - 8$

Ⓒ $f^{-1}(x) = -5x + 40$

Ⓓ $f^{-1}(x) = 5x + 40$

Ⓔ $f^{-1}(x) = -5x - 40$

2. *Multiple Choice* Which function is the inverse of $f(x) = 3x - 10$?

Ⓐ $f^{-1}(x) = \frac{1}{3}x + 10$

Ⓑ $f^{-1}(x) = -\frac{1}{3}x + 10$

Ⓒ $f^{-1}(x) = -3x - 10$

Ⓓ $f^{-1}(x) = -3x + 10$

Ⓔ $f^{-1}(x) = \frac{1}{3}x + \frac{10}{3}$

3. *Multiple Choice* Which function is the inverse of $f(x) = \frac{1}{4}x^3 + 1$?

Ⓐ $f^{-1}(x) = \sqrt[3]{4x}$

Ⓑ $f^{-1}(x) = \sqrt[3]{x - 1}$

Ⓒ $f^{-1}(x) = \sqrt[3]{4x - 4}$

Ⓓ $f^{-1}(x) = \sqrt[3]{4x - 1}$

Ⓔ $f^{-1}(x) = \sqrt[3]{4x + 4}$

4. *Multiple Choice* Which of the following has an inverse function?

Ⓐ $f(x) = x^2$ Ⓑ $f(x) = 2x^3$

Ⓒ $f(x) = x^4 + 1$ Ⓓ $f(x) = 3x^4$

Ⓔ $f(x) = -x^6 - 4$

Quantitative Comparison **In Exercises 5–7, choose the statement below that is true about the given quantities.**

Ⓐ The number in column A is greater.

Ⓑ The number in column B is greater.

Ⓒ The two numbers are equal.

Ⓓ The relationship cannot be determined from the given information.

	Column A	Column B
5.	$f^{-1}(2)$ where $f(x) = 2x - 3$	$f^{-1}(-1)$ where $f(x) = 5x + 4$
6.	$f^{-1}(-7)$ where $f(x) = x^3 + 1$	$f^{-1}(-6)$ where $f(x) = -x^3 + 2$
7.	$f^{-1}(-42)$ where $f(x) = -2x^5 + 22$	$f^{-1}(26)$ where $f(x) = x^5 - 6$

8. *Multiple Choice* Which of the following pairs are inverse functions?

Ⓐ $f(x) = 5x^{1/2}$ Ⓑ $f(x) = \frac{1}{2}x^4$

   $g(x) = \frac{x^2}{5}$ $g(x) = 2\sqrt[4]{x}$

Ⓒ $f(x) = 6x^{2/3}$ Ⓓ $f(x) = 27x^3$

   $g(x) = \left(\frac{x}{6}\right)^{2/3}$ $g(x) = \frac{x^{1/3}}{3}$

Ⓔ $f(x) = -x^5$

   $g(x) = \sqrt[5]{x}$

Chapter 7

Standardized Test Practice

For use with pages 431–436

TEST TAKING STRATEGY   **When taking a test, go back and answer questions that you suspect will take you extra time and effort.**

1. **Multiple Choice**   Which function is graphed?

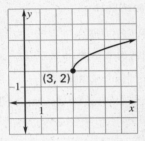

(3, 2)

Ⓐ $y = \sqrt{x} + 3$

Ⓑ $y = \sqrt{x - 3} + 2$

Ⓒ $y = \sqrt{x - 3} - 2$

Ⓓ $y = \sqrt{x + 3} - 2$

Ⓔ $y = \sqrt{x - 3}$

2. **Multiple Choice**   Which function is graphed?

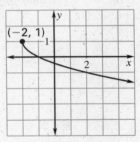

(−2, 1)

Ⓐ $y = \sqrt{x + 2} + 1$

Ⓑ $y = -\sqrt{x + 2}$

Ⓒ $y = \sqrt{x + 2}$

Ⓓ $y = -\sqrt{x + 2} + 1$

Ⓔ $y = -\sqrt{x + 2} - 1$

3. **Multiple Choice**   Which is the domain and range of $y = -6\sqrt{x + 3} - 8$?

Ⓐ $x \geq -3, y \leq 8$

Ⓑ $x \geq 3, y \leq -8$

Ⓒ $x \geq -3, y \leq -8$

Ⓓ $x \geq -3, y \geq -8$

Ⓔ $x \geq -3, y \geq 8$

4. **Multiple Choice**   Which is the domain and range of $y = 5\sqrt{x - 1} + 3$?

Ⓐ $x \geq 1, y \geq 3$

Ⓑ $x \geq 1, y \leq 3$

Ⓒ $x \geq -1, y \leq -3$

Ⓓ $x \leq 1, y \geq 3$

Ⓔ $x \leq 1, y \geq -3$

5. **Multi-Step Problem**   The fetch f (in nautical miles) of the wind at sea is the distance over which the wind is blowing. The minimum fetch required to create a fully developed storm can be modeled by

$$s = 3.1\sqrt[3]{f + 10} + 11.1$$

where s is the speed (in knots) of the wind.

   a. Graph the model.

   b. Determine the wind speed if the minimum fetch is 92.42 nautical miles.

   c. Determine the minimum fetch required to create a fully developed storm if the wind speed is 28 knots.

   d. *Writing*   Using the model graphed in part (a) explain whether a fully developed storm is created if the wind speed is 24 knots and the fetch is 80 nautical miles.

Standardized Test Practice

For use with pages 437–444

TEST TAKING STRATEGY   **Try to find shortcuts that will help you move through the questions quicker.**

1. *Multiple Choice* What is the solution of the equation $3\sqrt[3]{x} + 4 = 12$?

  (A) 12   (B) 40

  (C) 60   (D) 85

  (E) 140

2. *Multiple Choice* What is the solution of the equation $(2x + 15)^{1/2} - 2 = 3$?

  (A) 0   (B) 5

  (C) −5   (D) 10

  (E) −10

3. *Multiple Choice* What is the solution of the equation $\sqrt{3x + 4} = 2 - \sqrt{x}$?

  (A) 0   (B) 2

  (C) 4   (D) −2

  (E) −4

4. *Multiple Choice* What is (are) the solution(s) of the equation $\sqrt{7 - 2x} = x - 2$?

  (A) −1, 3   (B) −1

  (C) ±1   (D) ±3

  (E) 3

5. *Multiple Choice* What is the solution of the equation $\sqrt[3]{120x + 30} = \sqrt[3]{240x - 10}$?

  (A) $\dfrac{1}{3}$ (B) 3

  (C) $\dfrac{2}{3}$ (D) $\dfrac{3}{2}$

  (E) $-\dfrac{1}{3}$

6. *Multiple Choice* What is the solution of the equation $\sqrt[4]{57 - 4x} = \sqrt[4]{69 - 2x}$?

  (A) $\dfrac{1}{6}$ (B) $-\dfrac{1}{6}$

  (C) 6   (D) −6

  (E) 2

Quantitative Comparison   **In Exercises 7–10, choose the statement below that is true about the given quantities.**

  (A) The number in column A is greater.

  (B) The number in column B is greater.

  (C) The two numbers are equal.

  (D) The relationship cannot be determined from the given information.

	Column A	Column B
7.	The solution of the equation $-4\sqrt{x + 1} = -16$	The solution of the equation $3\sqrt{x + 2} = 12$
8.	The solution of the equation $\sqrt[3]{6x - 1} = \sqrt[3]{2x + 9}$	The solution of the equation $\sqrt[3]{9 - 4x} = \sqrt[3]{7x - 2}$
9.	The solution of the equation $2x^{5/2} = 2048$	The solution of the equation $\sqrt{6x - 32} = 8$
10.	The solution of the equation $\sqrt{\dfrac{x}{2}} = 8$	The solution of the equation $\sqrt[3]{\dfrac{2x}{3}} = 5$

Chapter 7

Algebra 2
Standardized Test Practice Workbook

63

Standardized Test Practice

For use with pages 445–454

TEST TAKING STRATEGY   **If you keep up your homework, both your problem-solving abilities and your vocabulary will improve.**

1. *Multiple Choice*   What is the mean of 2, 3.6, 4, 5.2, 6, 8, 10, 12.4?

   (A) 6.1   (B) 6.4   (C) 6.2
   (D) 6.8   (E) 6.5

2. *Multiple Choice*   What is the mean of 7.4, 9.6, 10.2, 10.8, 14.6, 14.6, 18, 25.2, 32.7?

   (A) 14.6   (B) 14.9   (C) 15.2
   (D) 15.6   (E) 15.9

3. *Multiple Choice*   What is the median of 8, 2, 10, 11, 1, 7, 3?

   (A) 11   (B) 8   (C) 7
   (D) 3   (E) 6.9

4. *Multiple Choice*   What is (are) the mode(s) of 4, 8, 6, 10, 6, 1, 2, 8, 11, 7, 6, 5, 1, 8?

   (A) 1, 6, 8   (B) 1, 8   (C) 6, 8
   (D) 8   (E) 6

5. *Multiple Choice*   What is the standard deviation of 8, 15, 18, 22, 30, 34?

   (A) 8.2   (B) 8.8   (C) 9.0
   (D) 9.1   (E) 9.4

6. *Multiple Choice*   Which data set matches the box-and-whisker plot shown?

   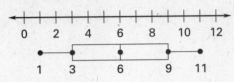

   (A) 1, 3, 3, 5, 8, 9, 11
   (B) 1, 2, 3, 4, 6, 9, 11
   (C) 1, 2, 5, 5, 6, 11
   (D) 1, 3, 4, 6, 8, 9, 11
   (E) 1, 2, 6, 6, 9, 9, 11

7. *Multi-Step Problem*   In an AP History course consisting of 18 students the following scores (100 possible points) were achieved on a comprehensive exam.

98	84	88	91	99	98
100	92	76	80	84	97
82	71	100	77	98	76

   a. Find the median.

   b. Find the mean.

   c. Find the standard deviation.

   d. Find the mode(s).

   e. Construct a box-and-whisker plot.

   f. *Writing*   National scores for this test range from a minimum of 58 to a maximum of 100. The median is 82, the lower quartile is 78, and the upper quartile is 86. Explain using the box-and-whisker plot from (e) whether these student scores are more spread out overall or more spread out about the mean as compared with the national scores.

Chapter 7

NAME _____ DATE _____

Cumulative Standardized Test Practice

For use after Chapter 7

1. *Multiple Choice* What is the value of $-125^{2/3}$?

   (A) 5   (B) -25 (C) 25

   (D) -5 (E) ± 25

2. *Multiple Choice* Which number is the solution of the equation $-4x - 13 = 11$?

   (A) -6 (B) $-\dfrac{1}{2}$ (C) 4

   (D) 6   (E) $\dfrac{1}{2}$

3. *Multiple Choice* What is the solution of $x^2 + 2x - 24 > 0$?

   (A) $x = -6$ or $x = 4$

   (B) $-6 < x < 4$

   (C) $x > -6$ or $x < 4$

   (D) $-4 < x < 6$

   (E) $x < -6$ or $x > 4$

4. *Multiple Choice* What is the slope of the line that passes through $(-10, 1)$ and $(5, -8)$?

   (A) $-\dfrac{5}{3}$ (B) $\dfrac{7}{5}$ (C) $-\dfrac{3}{5}$

   (D) $\dfrac{5}{3}$ (E) $\dfrac{3}{5}$

5. *Multiple Choice* What are the zeros of $f(x) = x^3 + x^2 - 16x + 20$?

   (A) 2   (B) 2, 5   (C) $i, \pm 5$

   (D) $\pm i, 2$ (E) $-5, 2$

6. *Multiple Choice* The variables x and y very directly, and $y = 34$ when $x = 17$. Which equation relates the variables?

   (A) $y = 17x$ (B) $y = \dfrac{1}{17}x$

   (C) $y = 34x$ (D) $y = 2x$

   (E) $y = \dfrac{1}{2}x$

7. *Multiple Choice* Which number does $(-6) - (-18)$ equal?

   (A) -24 (B) 12   (C) 24

   (D) -12 (E) 108

8. *Multiple Choice* Which matrix is the solution matrix of the linear system?

   $$-3x + 2y = -24$$
   $$5x - y = 26$$

   (A) $\begin{bmatrix} 4 \\ 6 \end{bmatrix}$ (B) $\begin{bmatrix} 6 \\ -4 \end{bmatrix}$ (C) $\begin{bmatrix} -4 \\ -6 \end{bmatrix}$

   (D) $\begin{bmatrix} 4 \\ -6 \end{bmatrix}$ (E) $\begin{bmatrix} -6 \\ 4 \end{bmatrix}$

9. *Multiple Choice* If you drive 528 miles and you average 16.5 miles per gallon, how much do you spend for gas if it costs $1.35 a gallon?

   (A) $43.00   (B) $43.15   (C) $43.20

   (D) $43.30   (E) $43.35

10. *Multiple Choice* If $f(x) = 2x - 3$ and $g(x) = x^2 - 2$, what is $g(f(x))$?

   (A) $4x^2 + 12x + 7$ (B) $2x^2 - 5$

   (C) $2x^2 - 7$ (D) $4x^2 - 6x + 7$

   (E) $4x^2 - 12x + 7$

Chapter 7

Quantitative Comparison **In Exercises 11–16, choose the statement below that is true about the given quantities.**

- (A) The number in column A is greater.
- (B) The number in column B is greater.
- (C) The two numbers are equal.
- (D) The relationship cannot be determined from the given information.

	Column A	Column B
11.	$4(3 - 8) + (-25) \div 5$	$-5 \times 10 - (14 - 39)$
12.	The value of x when $4x - 13 = -2x + 5$	The value of x when $3(x - 1) = -x - 11$
13.	$f(x) = x^2 - 3x + 1$ when $x = -2$	$f(x) = 2x^2 + x - 3$ when $x = -2$
14.	x-intercept of $2x + 3y = -12$	slope of $-20x + 5y = 10$
15.	$\det \begin{bmatrix} -2 & 6 \\ 1 & 7 \end{bmatrix}$	$\det \begin{bmatrix} 2 & 5 \\ -1 & -3 \end{bmatrix}$
16.	$(-2)^{-3}(5)^{-2}$	$-(5)^{-2}(64)^{-1/2}$

17. *Multiple Choice* What is the vertex of the graph of $y = -2(x + 1)(x - 3)$?

- (A) $(4, 10)$
- (B) $(1, -8)$
- (C) $(-1, 8)$
- (D) $(4, -10)$
- (E) $(1, 8)$

18. *Multiple Choice* Which cubic function models the data shown?

- (A) $f(x) = x^3 - 2x^2 + 5x - 7$
- (B) $f(x) = x^3 + 2x^2 - 5x - 7$
- (C) $f(x) = x^3 - 2x^2 + 5x + 7$
- (D) $f(x) = -x^3 - 2x^2 - 5x - 7$
- (E) $f(x) = -x^3 - 2x^2 + 5x + 7$

19. *Multiple Choice* Which function is the inverse of $f(x) = -4x + 15$?

- (A) $f^{-1}(x) = \frac{1}{4}x + 15$
- (B) $f^{-1}(x) = -4x + 15$
- (C) $f^{-1}(x) = -4x - 15$
- (D) $f^{-1}(x) = -\frac{1}{4}x + \frac{15}{4}$
- (E) $f^{-1}(x) = \frac{1}{4}x + \frac{15}{4}$

20. *Multiple Choice* Which inequality is a solution of $-5(x - 2) \geq x - 14$?

- (A) $x \leq 4$
- (B) $x \geq 1$
- (C) $x \geq -4$
- (D) $x \geq 4$
- (E) $x \leq -1$

21. *Multiple Choice* Which inequality is represented by the graph shown?

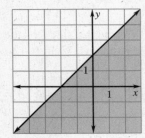

- (A) $y > -x + 2$
- (B) $y \geq x - 2$
- (C) $y < x + 2$
- (D) $y \leq x + 2$
- (E) $y < -x - 2$

22. *Multiple Choice* $(2x - 3)^3 = \underline{\ \ ?\ \ }$

- (A) $8x^3 + 36x^2 + 54x + 27$
- (B) $8x^3 - 36x^2 - 54x - 27$
- (C) $8x^3 - 36x^2 + 54x - 27$
- (D) $8x^3 + 36x^2 - 54x + 27$
- (E) $-8x^3 + 36x^2 - 54x + 27$

Chapter 7

Algebra 2
Standardized Test Practice Workbook

23. *Multiple Choice* Which ordered pair is a solution of the following system of linear equations?

$$x + 2y = 11$$
$$-2x - 3y = -16$$

Ⓐ (6, 1)   Ⓑ (−1, 6)

Ⓒ (1, 6)   Ⓓ (−1, −6)

Ⓔ (−6, 1)

24. *Multi-Step Problem* You are selling two types of candy assortments. One type costs $2.50 for each box and the other type costs $3.00 for each box.

a. Let x represent one type of candy and let y represent the other type. Write a model that expresses the total number of boxes and another which represents the amount of income made from selling all of the boxes.

b. You have a total of 65 boxes to sell and your team leader would like you to raise at least $182.50. Write a system of linear equations and solve the system to determine the amount of each type of candy you will need to sell.

c. Graph the system of equations from part (b) on the same graph. Estimate the coordinates of the point where the two graphs intersect.

d. *Writing* Explain which method would be best to use in determining the amount of each type of candy to sell.

25. *Multiple Choice* At which point does the graph of $6x - 3y - 8z = 24$ cross the z-axis?

Ⓐ (0, 0, 3)   Ⓑ (4, 0, 0)

Ⓒ (−4, 0, 0)   Ⓓ (0, −8, 0)

Ⓔ (0, 0, −3)

26. *Multiple Choice* What does the product $(2 - 3i)(5 + 8i)$ equal?

Ⓐ $10 - 24i^2$ Ⓑ $34 + i$

Ⓒ $34 - 31i$ Ⓓ $-34 + i$

Ⓔ $34 + 31i$

27. *Multiple Choice* What type of polynomial function is $f(x) = -2x^3 + 5x^2 - 7x + 32$?

Ⓐ constant   Ⓑ linear

Ⓒ quadratic   Ⓓ cubic

Ⓔ quartic

28. *Multiple Choice* What is $\sqrt[6]{4} \cdot \sqrt[6]{16}$?

Ⓐ −2   Ⓑ 2   Ⓒ −3

Ⓓ 3   Ⓔ 4

29. *Multiple Choice* Which of the following is the factorization of $x^3 + 10x^2 + 12x - 72$?

Ⓐ $(x - 2)(x + 2)(x + 6)$

Ⓑ $(x - 6)^2(x + 2)$

Ⓒ $(x - 2)(x + 6)^2$

Ⓓ $(x - 6)(x + 6)(x - 2)$

Ⓔ $(x + 6)^2(x + 2)$

30. *Multiple Choice* What are all solutions of $2x^2 + 5(3x - 4) = 5x^2 - 6x + 10$?

Ⓐ 2   Ⓑ 5   Ⓒ −2

Ⓓ −2, 5   Ⓔ 2, 5

31. *Multiple Choice* Which matrix equals

$$-4\begin{bmatrix} 1 & -5 \\ -1 & 8 \end{bmatrix} - 3\begin{bmatrix} 7 & -9 \\ 0 & 6 \end{bmatrix}?$$

Ⓐ $\begin{bmatrix} -25 & 47 \\ 4 & -50 \end{bmatrix}$ Ⓑ $\begin{bmatrix} -17 & 47 \\ 7 & -50 \end{bmatrix}$

Ⓒ $\begin{bmatrix} 17 & 47 \\ -1 & -50 \end{bmatrix}$ Ⓓ $\begin{bmatrix} 25 & -47 \\ 4 & -50 \end{bmatrix}$

Ⓔ $\begin{bmatrix} -25 & 47 \\ -4 & -50 \end{bmatrix}$

Chapter 7

32. Multiple Choice A ladder 30 feet in length that hits the wall at a height of 24 feet has a slope of ___?___ .

(A) $\dfrac{3}{4}$ (B) $\dfrac{4}{3}$ (C) $\dfrac{3}{5}$

(D) $\dfrac{5}{3}$ (E) $\dfrac{4}{5}$

Quantitative Comparison **In Exercises 33–38, choose the statement below that is true about the given quantities.**

(A) The number in column A is greater.

(B) The number in column B is greater.

(C) The two numbers are equal.

(D) The relationship cannot be determined from the given information.

	Column A	Column B
33.	$\sqrt[4]{3} \cdot \sqrt[4]{12}$	$\sqrt[6]{25} \cdot \sqrt[6]{5}$
34.	solution of $x^2 + 8x = -16$	solution of $x^2 - 12x + 16 = -20$
35.	$y = -2|x - 2| + 1$ when $x = -3$	$y = 3|x| - 15$ when $x = -2$
36.	-4	the y-coordinate of the solution of $2x + 3y = 8$ $-5x + 2y = -1$
37.	$f(x, y) = 3x - 5y + 4$ at $f(-1, 2)$	$f(x, y) = 3x - 5y + 4$ at $f(-5, 2)$
38.	solution of $4x + 8y = -12$	$y = 2$

39. Multiple Choice What is $f(x) = 5x^5 - 3x^4 - 2x^3 - x^2 - 4x + 11$ when $x = 2$?

(A) 131 (B) -95 (C) 97

(D) 95 (E) -97

40. Multiple Choice What is the solution of the equation $\sqrt{2x - 3} = 7 - \sqrt{3x - 2}$?

(A) 4 (B) 2 (C) -6

(D) -4 (E) 6

Chapter 7

TEST TAKING STRATEGY   **The best way to prepare for a standardized test is to keep up with your day to day studies.**

1. *Multiple Choice*   Which function is graphed?

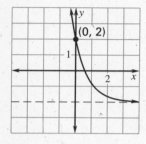

Ⓐ $f(x) = 4(0.3)^x - 2$

Ⓑ $f(x) = 4(0.3)^x$

Ⓒ $f(x) = 4(0.3)^{x-2}$

Ⓓ $f(x) = -4(0.3)^{x-2}$

Ⓔ $f(x) = -4(0.3)^x - 2$

2. *Multiple Choice*   Which function is graphed?

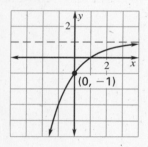

Ⓐ $f(x) = -2(0.5)^{x+1}$

Ⓑ $f(x) = 2(0.5)^x$

Ⓒ $f(x) = 2(0.5)^x - 1$

Ⓓ $f(x) = -2(0.5)^x + 1$

Ⓔ $f(x) = 2(0.5)^x + 1$

3. *Multiple Choice*   What is the range of $y = 5(3)^{x-2} - 1$?

Ⓐ $y > 5$ Ⓑ $y < 1$

Ⓒ $y > -1$ Ⓓ $y < 3$

Ⓔ $y > 3$

4. *Multiple Choice*   Suppose you deposit $10,000 in an account that pays 7% annual interest. What is the balance after three years if the interest is compounded monthly?

Ⓐ $12,100.45   Ⓑ $12,329.26

Ⓒ $12,251.13   Ⓓ $12,862.94

Ⓔ $12,914.55

5. *Multi-Step Problem*   A local bank advertises two special savings accounts. You have $500 and you want to decide which offer is the best investment.

a. One account offers 4.9% compounded daily. Write a formula that gives the balance of this account at the end of one year.

b. The other account offers 5% compounded quarterly. Write a formula that gives the balance of this account at the end of one year.

c. Determine the balance of the account using the formula from part (a).

d. Determine the balance of the account using the formula from part (b).

e. *Writing*   Explain which account is the best investment and whether the interest rate or compounding period is of more importance.

Chapter 8

Standardized Test Practice

For use with pages 474–479

TEST TAKING STRATEGY   **If you use the same method to find and check an answer, you may make the same mistake twice.**

1. **Multiple Choice**   Which of the following is an exponential decay function?

   Ⓐ $f(x) = 4(2)^x$ Ⓑ $f(x) = 3\left(\frac{4}{3}\right)^{-x}$

   Ⓒ $f(x) = 5\left(\frac{1}{3}\right)^{-x}$ Ⓓ $f(x) = 6\left(\frac{4}{5}\right)^{-x}$

   Ⓔ $f(x) = 3\left(\frac{6}{5}\right)^{x}$

2. **Multiple Choice**   Which of the following is an exponential decay function?

   Ⓐ $f(x) = 4\left(\frac{2}{3}\right)^{-x}$ Ⓑ $f(x) = 3^x$

   Ⓒ $f(x) = 7\left(\frac{2}{5}\right)^{-x}$ Ⓓ $f(x) = 2(5)^{-x}$

   Ⓔ $f(x) = 8\left(\frac{8}{3}\right)^{x}$

3. **Multiple Choice**   Which function is graphed?

   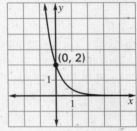

   (0, 2)

   1

   1

   Ⓐ $f(x) = 2\left(\frac{1}{5}\right)^{-x}$ Ⓑ $f(x) = \left(\frac{1}{5}\right)^{x}$

   Ⓒ $f(x) = -2\left(\frac{1}{5}\right)^{x}$ Ⓓ $f(x) = 2\left(\frac{1}{5}\right)^{x}$

   Ⓔ $f(x) = 2(5)^{x}$

4. **Multiple Choice**   What is the range of the graph $y = 5\left(\frac{1}{4}\right)^{x+1} + 2$?

   Ⓐ $y > 2$ Ⓑ $y < -2$

   Ⓒ $y < 5$ Ⓓ $y > 5$

   Ⓔ $y < 2$

5. **Multiple Choice**   What is the range of the graph $y = (0.3)^{x-2} - 3$?

   Ⓐ $y > 3$ Ⓑ $y < -0.3$

   Ⓒ $y < 0.3$ Ⓓ $y > -3$

   Ⓔ $y < 3$

6. **Multi-Step Problem**   You have bought a new car for $26,500. The value y of the car decreases by 18% each year.

   a. Write an exponential decay model for the value of the car.

   b. Use the model to estimate the value of the car after three years.

   c. Graph the model.

   d. Use the graph to estimate when the car will have a value of $18,000.

   e. **Writing**   Explain if there is a point at which the car will have almost no value.

Chapter 8

Standardized Test Practice

For use with pages 480–485

TEST TAKING STRATEGY **During a test, draw graphs and figures in your test booklet to help you solve problems.**

1. *Multiple Choice* What is the simplified form of $e^5 \cdot e^{-3}$?

Ⓐ e^{-15} Ⓑ $2e^{-15}$ Ⓒ $2e^2$

Ⓓ e^2 Ⓔ e^{-2}

2. *Multiple Choice* What is the simplified form of $\dfrac{-16e^7}{2e^4}$?

Ⓐ $-8e^3$ Ⓑ $8e^{28}$

Ⓒ $-8e^{-3}$ Ⓓ $-8e^{28}$

Ⓔ $-8e^{7/4}$

3. *Multiple Choice* What is the simplified form of $(-4e^{-6x})^2$?

Ⓐ $4e^{12x^2}$ Ⓑ $8e^{12x}$

Ⓒ $-8e^{-36x}$ Ⓓ $\dfrac{16}{e^{12x}}$

Ⓔ $\dfrac{16}{e^{12x}}$

4. *Multiple Choice* What is the simplified form of $5e^{-8} \cdot (-2e^3)^2$?

Ⓐ $-10e^{-40}$ Ⓑ $-20e^2$ Ⓒ $\dfrac{20}{e^2}$

Ⓓ $\dfrac{20}{e^{48}}$ Ⓔ $\dfrac{10}{e^2}$

5. *Multiple Choice* What is the range of the function $y = e^{-2(x+1)} - 3$?

Ⓐ $y > 3$ Ⓑ $y < 3$

Ⓒ $y > -2$ Ⓓ $y < -2$

Ⓔ $y > -3$

Quantitative Comparison **In Exercises 6–8, choose the statement below that is true about the given quantities.**

Ⓐ The number in column A is greater.

Ⓑ The number in column B is greater.

Ⓒ The two numbers are equal.

Ⓓ The relationship cannot be determined from the given information.

	Column A	Column B
6.	e^4	$2e^{-3}$
7.	$(2e^2)^3$	$\dfrac{1}{\left(\sqrt{8}(e^3)\right)^{-2}}$
8.	$(-5e^{-4})^2$	$(5e^4)^{-2}$

9. *Multiple Choice* What is the range of the function $f(x) = 3e^{0.5(x-2)} + 4$?

Ⓐ $y < 4$ Ⓑ $y > 4$

Ⓒ $y > -0.5$ Ⓓ $y < -1$

Ⓔ $y < -4$

10. *Multiple Choice* If you deposit $2000 in an account that pays 6.5% annual interest compounded continuously, what is the balance after three years?

Ⓐ $2,134.32   Ⓑ $5,835.96

Ⓒ $2,415.90   Ⓓ $2,168.51

Ⓔ $2,430.62

Chapter 8

Standardized Test Practice

For use with pages 486–492

TEST TAKING STRATEGY   **Long-term preparation will definitely affect not only your standardized test scores, but your overall future academic performance as well.**

1. *Multiple Choice*   Which of the following is equivalent to $\log_5 125$?

   Ⓐ 25   Ⓑ $\frac{1}{5}$ Ⓒ 3

   Ⓓ 5   Ⓔ $\frac{1}{3}$

2. *Multiple Choice*   Which of the following is equivalent to $\log_{0.25} 16$?

   Ⓐ $\frac{1}{4}$ Ⓑ -4 Ⓒ 2

   Ⓓ -2 Ⓔ $-\frac{1}{4}$

3. *Multiple Choice*   Which of the following is equivalent to $\log_4 64^x$?

   Ⓐ 4^{3x} Ⓑ 3^x Ⓒ $4x$

   Ⓓ $\frac{1}{4}x$ Ⓔ $3x$

4. *Multiple Choice*   What is the inverse of the function $y = \log_5 x$?

   Ⓐ $y = 5^x$ Ⓑ $y = 5x$

   Ⓒ $y = \frac{1}{5}x$ Ⓓ $y = x^5$

   Ⓔ $y = \frac{1}{5^x}$

5. *Multiple Choice*   What is the inverse of the function $y = \ln(x + 3)$?

   Ⓐ $y = 3^x - e$ Ⓑ $y = x^3 - e$

   Ⓒ $y = e^x - 3$ Ⓓ $y = e^3 - x$

   Ⓔ $y = e^{3x}$

6. *Multiple Choice*   What is the domain of the function $y = \log_3(x - 7)$?

   Ⓐ $x > 7$ Ⓑ $x < 7$

   Ⓒ $-7 \le x \le 7$ Ⓓ $x \ge 7$

   Ⓔ $x \le 7$

7. *Multiple Choice*   What is the domain of the function $y = \log_{0.2}(x + 2)$?

   Ⓐ $x \ge -2$ Ⓑ $x < -2$

   Ⓒ $-2 \le x \le 2$ Ⓓ $x > -2$

   Ⓔ $x \le -2$

Quantitative Comparison   **In Exercises 8–10, choose the statement below that is true about the given quantities.**

   Ⓐ   The number in column A is greater.

   Ⓑ   The number in column B is greater.

   Ⓒ   The two numbers are equal.

   Ⓓ   The relationship cannot be determined from the given information.

	Column A	*Column B*
8.	$\log_6 216$	$\log_3 27$
9.	$f\left(\frac{1}{16}\right)$ where $f(x) = \log_4 x$	-1
10.	$f(-2)$ where $f(x) = \log_3 3^x$	-2

Standardized Test Practice

For use with pages 493–499

TEST TAKING STRATEGY **Draw an arrow on your test booklet next to questions that you do not answer. This will enable you to find the questions quickly when you go back.**

1. *Multiple Choice* What is the approximation of $\log_6 \frac{2}{8}$?

   Ⓐ 0.774 Ⓑ 1.723

   Ⓒ −1.547 Ⓓ 0.646

   Ⓔ −0.774

2. *Multiple Choice* What is the approximation of $\log_{1/2} 28$?

   Ⓐ −0.208 Ⓑ −4.807

   Ⓒ 0.807 Ⓓ −12.099

   Ⓔ 8.099

3. *Multiple Choice* Which of the following is equivalent to $\log \frac{x^2 y^3}{z^4}$?

   Ⓐ $6 \log xy - 4 \log z$

   Ⓑ $2 \log x - 3 \log y + 4 \log z$

   Ⓒ $2 \log x + 3 \log y + 4 \log z$

   Ⓓ $2 \log x + 3 \log y - 4 \log z$

   Ⓔ $3 \log y - 2 \log x - 4 \log z$

4. *Multiple Choice* What is the condensed expression for $3 \log x - \log 2$?

   Ⓐ $\log \frac{x^3}{2}$ Ⓑ $\log 2x^3$

   Ⓒ $\log 2x^{-3}$ Ⓓ $\log \frac{x^{-3}}{2}$

   Ⓔ $\log -2x^{-3}$

5. *Multiple Choice* What is the condensed expression for $2 \ln x + \ln 3$?

   Ⓐ $3 \ln x^2$ Ⓑ $\ln \frac{x^2}{3}$

   Ⓒ $\ln 3x^2$ Ⓓ $\ln \frac{3}{x^2}$

   Ⓔ $x^2 \ln 3$

Quantitative Comparison **In Exercises 6–8, choose the statement below that is true about the given quantities.**

   Ⓐ The number in column A is greater.

   Ⓑ The number in column B is greater.

   Ⓒ The two numbers are equal.

   Ⓓ The relationship cannot be determined from the given information.

	Column A	Column B
6.	$\ln e^{-2}$	$\log 0.01$
7.	$\ln x$	$\log_3 x$
8.	$\ln e^6$	$\log_4 1024$

9. *Multiple Choice* Which of the following is *not* correct?

   Ⓐ $\log_2 4 + \log_2 9 = \log_2 36$

   Ⓑ $\log_2 18 + \log_2 18 = \log_2 36$

   Ⓒ $\log_2 3 + \log_2 12 = \log_2 36$

   Ⓓ $\log_2 6 + \log_2 6 = \log_2 36$

   Ⓔ $\log_2 2 + \log_2 18 = \log_2 36$

Standardized Test Practice

For use with pages 501–508

TEST TAKING STRATEGY **If you get stuck on a question, look at the answer choices for clues.**

1. *Multiple Choice* What is the solution of $4^{4x} = 16^{x+1}$?

  Ⓐ 0 Ⓑ 1 Ⓒ 2
  Ⓓ 3 Ⓔ 4

2. *Multiple Choice* What is the solution of $3^x = 45$?

  Ⓐ 3.338 Ⓑ 3.382 Ⓒ 3.417
  Ⓓ 3.438 Ⓔ 3.465

3. *Multiple Choice* What is the solution of $5^{x-2} + 3 = 32$?

  Ⓐ 4.085 Ⓑ 4.092 Ⓒ 4.096
  Ⓓ 4.099 Ⓔ 4.102

4. *Multiple Choice* What is the solution of $\log_6 (2x - 7) = \log_6 (x - 3)$?

  Ⓐ −1 Ⓑ 0 Ⓒ 1
  Ⓓ 2 Ⓔ 4

5. *Multiple Choice* What is the solution of $\log_7 (4x + 5) = 2$?

  Ⓐ 2 Ⓑ 6 Ⓒ 9
  Ⓓ 11 Ⓔ 14

Quantitative Comparison **In Exercises 6–8, choose the statement below that is true about the given quantities.**

  Ⓐ The number in column A is greater.
  Ⓑ The number in column B is greater.
  Ⓒ The two numbers are equal.
  Ⓓ The relationship cannot be determined from the given information.

	Column A	Column B
6.	$5^x = 10$	$3^x = 12$
7.	$2^{x+1} = 4^{x-2}$	$5^{3x} = 25^{x+1}$
8.	$\log_4 (x + 2) = 2$	$\log_3 (x - 5) = 2$

9. *Multiple Choice* What is the extraneous solution found in solving the equation $\log_2 4x + \log_2 (x + 1) = 3$?

  Ⓐ −2 Ⓑ −1 Ⓒ 1
  Ⓓ 2 Ⓔ −3

10. *Multiple Choice* What is the extraneous solution found in solving the equation $\log_6 2x + \log_6 (x + 3) = 2$?

  Ⓐ −3 Ⓑ $\frac{1}{2}$ Ⓒ 6
  Ⓓ 3 Ⓔ −6

Chapter 8

LESSON
8.7

NAME _____

DATE _____

Standardized Test Practice
For use with pages 509–516

TEST TAKING STRATEGY **During the test, do not worry excessively about how much time you have left. Concentrate on the question in front of you.**

1. *Multiple Choice* Which function passes through the points $(0, 5)$ and $(2, 45)$?

   Ⓐ $y = 2 \cdot 3^x$ Ⓑ $y = 5 \cdot 3^x$

   Ⓒ $y = 3 \cdot 5^x$ Ⓓ $y = 3 \cdot 2^x$

   Ⓔ $y = 5 \cdot 2^x$

2. *Multiple Choice* Which function passes through the points $(1, 0.5)$ and $(2, 1.5)$?

   Ⓐ $y = \dfrac{1}{2} \cdot 6^x$ Ⓑ $y = \dfrac{1}{3} \cdot 6^x$

   Ⓒ $y = \dfrac{1}{6} \cdot 3^x$ Ⓓ $y = \dfrac{1}{6} \cdot 2^x$

   Ⓔ $y = \dfrac{1}{3} \cdot 2^x$

3. *Multiple Choice* Which function passes through the points $(0, 0)$ and $(3, 3)$?

   Ⓐ $y = \dfrac{2}{3}x^2$ Ⓑ $y = \dfrac{1}{3}x^2$

   Ⓒ $y = \dfrac{2}{5}x^3$ Ⓓ $y = \dfrac{2}{3}x^3$

   Ⓔ $y = \dfrac{1}{5}x^2$

4. *Multiple Choice* Which function passes through the points $\left(1, \dfrac{2}{3}\right)$ and $(3, 18)$?

   Ⓐ $y = \dfrac{2}{3}x^2$ Ⓑ $y = \dfrac{1}{3}x^2$

   Ⓒ $y = \dfrac{2}{5}x^3$ Ⓓ $y = \dfrac{1}{3}x^3$

   Ⓔ $y = \dfrac{2}{3}x^3$

5. *Multiple Choice* Which function passes through the points $(1, 2.5)$ and $(3, 3.84)$?

   Ⓐ $y = 2.5x^{0.1}$ Ⓑ $y = 2.5x^{0.23}$

   Ⓒ $y = 2.5x^{0.28}$ Ⓓ $y = 2.5x^{0.35}$

   Ⓔ $y = 2.5x^{0.39}$

6. *Multiple Choice* Which function passes through the points $(1, 5.1)$ and $(4, 8.64)$?

   Ⓐ $y = 5.1x^{0.2}$ Ⓑ $y = 5.1x^{0.3}$

   Ⓒ $y = 5.1x^{0.38}$ Ⓓ $y = 5.1x^{0.32}$

   Ⓔ $y = 5.1x^{0.15}$

Quantitative Comparison **In Exercises 7–9, choose the statement below that is true about the given quantities.**

   Ⓐ The number in column A is greater.

   Ⓑ The number in column B is greater.

   Ⓒ The two numbers are equal.

   Ⓓ The relationship cannot be determined from the given information.

	Column A	Column B
7.	$f(3)$ where $f(x) = 2 \cdot 5^x$	$f(2)$ where $f(x) = 3 \cdot 6^x$
8.	$f(2)$ where $f(x) = 4x^{0.32}$	$f(4)$ where $f(x) = 7x^{0.14}$
9.	$f(3)$ where $f(x) = 3x^{1.2}$	$f(4)$ where $f(x) = 3x^{1.2}$

Chapter 8

Some college entrance exams allow the optional use of calculators. If you do use a calculator, make sure it is one you are familiar with and have used before.

1. *Multiple Choice* What is $f(-3)$ where

$$f(x) = \frac{50}{1 + 7e^{-x}}?$$

Ⓐ 0.3342   Ⓑ 0.3487

Ⓒ 0.3531   Ⓓ 0.3672

Ⓔ 0.3915

2. *Multiple Choice* What is $f(2)$ where

$$f(x) = \frac{6}{1 + 5e^{-3x}}?$$

Ⓐ 5.76   Ⓑ 5.81   Ⓒ 5.83

Ⓓ 5.88   Ⓔ 5.93

3. *Multiple Choice* What is the solution of the equation

$$\frac{30}{1 + 6e^{-5x}} = 10?$$

Ⓐ 0.15   Ⓑ 0.18   Ⓒ 0.22

Ⓓ 0.27   Ⓔ 0.31

4. *Multiple Choice* What is the solution of the equation

$$\frac{15}{2 + 5e^{-2x}} = 6?$$

Ⓐ 1.15   Ⓑ 1.24   Ⓒ 1.28

Ⓓ 1.29   Ⓔ 1.36

5. *Multiple Choice* Which function is graphed?

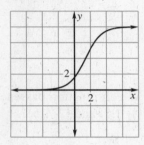

Ⓐ $f(x) = \dfrac{8}{1 + 4e^x}$

Ⓑ $f(x) = \dfrac{8}{1 + 4e^{-x}}$

Ⓒ $f(x) = \dfrac{8}{1 - 4e^{-x}}$

Ⓓ $f(x) = \dfrac{8}{1 - 4e^x}$

Ⓔ $f(x) = -\dfrac{8}{1 + 4e^{-x}}$

6. *Multi-Step Problem* Use the function

$$f(x) = \frac{7}{1 + 5e^{-x}}.$$

  a. Find $f(-2), f(0),$ and $f(3)$.

  b. Sketch the graph.

  c. Identify the asymptotes, y-intercept, and point of maximum growth.

  d. Write and solve an equation to find the value of x when $f(x)$ equals 6. Label this point on your graph.

  e. *Writing* Describe how the growth represented by this function changes over time.

Chapter 8

Standardized Test Practice

For use with pages 534–539

TEST TAKING STRATEGY **Read the test questions carefully.**

1. *Multiple Choice* The variable x varies inversely with y. When $x = 15$, $y = 1.2$. Which equation relates x and y?

   Ⓐ $y = 12.5x$ Ⓑ $xy = \dfrac{2}{25}$

   Ⓒ $xy = 18$ Ⓓ $y = 18x$

   Ⓔ $xy = 12.5$

2. *Multiple Choice* The variable x varies inversely with y. When $x = 0.25$, $y = 1.6$. Which equation relates x and y?

   Ⓐ $xy = 4$ Ⓑ $y = 0.4x$

   Ⓒ $xy = 0.15625$ Ⓓ $xy = 0.4$

   Ⓔ $y = 0.15625x$

3. *Multiple Choice* The variable z varies jointly with x and y. When $x = 10$ and $y = \frac{1}{2}$, $z = 45$. Which equation relates x, y, and z?

   Ⓐ $z = 45xy$ Ⓑ $z = 9xy$

   Ⓒ $z = \dfrac{1}{9}xy$ Ⓓ $z = \dfrac{1}{45}xy$

   Ⓔ $xyz = 45$

4. *Multiple Choice* The variable z varies directly with y and inversely with x. When $x = 4$ and $y = 28$, $z = 56$. Which equation relates x, y, and z?

   Ⓐ $z = 56xy$ Ⓑ $z = 8xy$

   Ⓒ $z = \dfrac{8y}{x}$ Ⓓ $z = \dfrac{xy}{56}$

   Ⓔ $z = \dfrac{56}{xy}$

Quantitative Comparison **In Exercises 5–7, choose the statement below that is true about the given quantities**

Ⓐ The number in column A is greater.

Ⓑ The number in column B is greater.

Ⓒ The two numbers are equal.

Ⓓ The relationship cannot be determined from the given information.

	Column A	*Column B*
5.	k where x varies directly with y; $y = 10$ when $x = 8$	k where x varies inversely with y; $y = 0.5$ when $x = 1.6$
6.	k where x varies inversely with y; $y = 5$ when $x = 3$	k where y varies inversely with x; $y = 30$ when $x = 0.5$
7.	k where z varies jointly with x and y; $z = 120$ and $y = 10$ when $x = 8$	k where z varies directly with x and y; $z = 15$ and $y = 5$ when $x = 25$

8. *Multiple Choice* The variable z varies jointly with x and y. When $x = 24$ and $y = 4$, $z = 120$. Which equation relates x, y, and z?

   Ⓐ $z = \dfrac{xy}{120}$ Ⓑ $z = 6xy$

   Ⓒ $z = \dfrac{5y}{4x}$ Ⓓ $xyz = 120$

   Ⓔ $z = 1.25xy$

NAME _____ DATE _____

Standardized Test Practice

For use with pages 540–545

TEST TAKING STRATEGY   **Do not panic if you run out of time before answering all of the questions. You can still receive a high score on a standardized test without answering every question.**

1. *Multiple Choice*   Which of the following is a function whose domain and range are all *nonzero* real numbers?

   Ⓐ $f(x) = \dfrac{6}{2x + 3}$ Ⓑ $f(x) = \dfrac{x - 1}{x + 5}$

   Ⓒ $f(x) = \dfrac{4x - 7}{x}$ Ⓓ $f(x) = \dfrac{x}{2x - 8}$

   Ⓔ   None of these

2. *Multiple Choice*   Which of the following is a function whose domain and range are all real numbers?

   Ⓐ $f(x) = \dfrac{x}{x - 3}$ Ⓑ $f(x) = \dfrac{2x - 9}{3}$

   Ⓒ $f(x) = \dfrac{3}{x} - 8$ Ⓓ $f(x) = \dfrac{5x + 2}{3x - 11}$

   Ⓔ   None of these

3. *Multiple Choice*   What are the asymptotes of the graph of $y = \dfrac{2}{x + 18} - 7$?

   Ⓐ $x = 18, y = 2$
   Ⓑ $x = -18, y = -7$
   Ⓒ $x = -18, y = 7$
   Ⓓ $x = 2, y = -18$
   Ⓔ $x = -7, y = -18$

4. *Multiple Choice*   What are the asymptotes of the graph of $y = \dfrac{3}{2x - 6} + 5$?

   Ⓐ $x = 3, y = 3$ Ⓑ $x = -3, y = -5$
   Ⓒ $x = 3, y = 5$ Ⓓ $x = 3, y = -5$
   Ⓔ $x = -5, y = 3$

5. *Multiple Choice*   What function is graphed?

   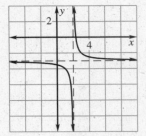

   Ⓐ $y = \dfrac{1}{x - 2} - 3$ Ⓑ $y = \dfrac{1}{x + 2} - 3$

   Ⓒ $y = \dfrac{1}{x - 2} + 3$ Ⓓ $y = \dfrac{1}{x + 2} + 3$

   Ⓔ   None of these

6. *Multiple-Step Problem*   For parts (a)–(d), graph the function and identify the point at which the horizontal and vertical asymptotes intersect.

   a. $y = \dfrac{3}{x}$ b. $y = \dfrac{3}{x - 2} + 1$

   c. $y = \dfrac{3}{x - 2} - 1$ d. $y = \dfrac{3}{x + 2} - 1$

   e. Use your answers to parts (a)–(d) to predict the point of intersection of the asymptotes of the graph of

   $$y = \dfrac{3}{x + 2} + 1.$$

   Check your prediction by graphing.

   f. *Critical Thinking*   Generalize your results for any function of the form

   $$y = \dfrac{a}{x - h} + k.$$

NAME _____ DATE _____

Standardized Test Practice

For use with pages 547–553

TEST TAKING STRATEGY **Long-term preparation will definitely affect not only your standardized test scores, but your overall future academic performance as well.**

1. *Multiple Choice* What is the range of the function $y = \dfrac{8}{x^2 + 2}$?

Ⓐ All real numbers   Ⓑ $0 \le y \le 8$

Ⓒ $0 < y \le 8$ Ⓓ $0 \le y \le 4$

Ⓔ $0 < y \le 4$

2. *Multiple Choice* What is the range of the function $y = \dfrac{-15}{x^2 + 5}$?

Ⓐ All real numbers   Ⓑ $-3 \le y < 0$

Ⓒ $0 < y \le 3$ Ⓓ $0 \le y \le 3$

Ⓔ $-3 < y \le 0$

3. *Multiple Choice* Which function is graphed?

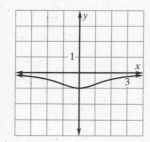

Ⓐ $y = \dfrac{-3}{x^2 - 3}$ Ⓑ $y = \dfrac{-3}{x^2 + 3}$

Ⓒ $y = \dfrac{3}{x^2 + 3}$ Ⓓ $y = \dfrac{-3}{(x - 3)^2}$

Ⓔ $y = \dfrac{3}{(x + 3)^2}$

4. *Multiple Choice* Which function is graphed?

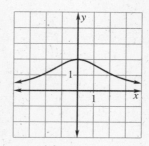

Ⓐ $y = \dfrac{-10}{x^2 - 5}$ Ⓑ $y = \dfrac{-10}{x^2 + 5}$

Ⓒ $y = \dfrac{10}{x^2 + 5}$ Ⓓ $y = \dfrac{-10}{(x - 5)^2}$

Ⓔ $y = \dfrac{10}{(x + 5)^2}$

5. *Multiple-Step Problem* The acceleration due to gravity g' (in meters per second squared) of a falling object at the moment it is dropped is given by the function

$$g' = \frac{3.99 \times 10^{14}}{h^2 + (1.28 \times 10^7)h + 4.07 \times 10^{13}}$$

where h is the object's altitude (in meters) above sea level.

a. Graph the function.

b. Find the acceleration due to gravity for an object dropped at an altitude of 3,500,000 meters.

c. *Critical Thinking* Explain how to use this function to find the acceleration due to gravity if the object's altitude is given in miles.

Standardized Test Practice

For use with pages 554–560

TEST TAKING STRATEGY   **During a test, draw graphs and figures in your test booklet to help you solve problems.**

1. *Multiple Choice*   What is the simplified form of $\dfrac{x^2 - 3x - 18}{x^2 - 36}$?

Ⓐ $\dfrac{x-2}{x+6}$ Ⓑ $\dfrac{x-3}{x-6}$

Ⓒ $\dfrac{x+3}{x-6}$ Ⓓ $\dfrac{x+3}{x+6}$

Ⓔ $\dfrac{x+2}{x-6}$

2. *Multiple Choice*   What is the product $\dfrac{x^2 - 3x - 10}{x^2 - 6x + 5} \cdot \dfrac{x-1}{x^2 - 4}$?

Ⓐ $x-2$ Ⓑ $\dfrac{1}{x-2}$

Ⓒ $x+2$ Ⓓ $\dfrac{1}{x+2}$

Ⓔ $\dfrac{x-1}{x-2}$

3. *Multiple Choice*   What is the quotient $(x+6) \div \dfrac{x^2 + 5x - 6}{x^2 + 7x - 8}$?

Ⓐ $x-1$ Ⓑ $\dfrac{x+8}{x+6}$

Ⓒ $\dfrac{x+6}{x+8}$ Ⓓ $x+6$

Ⓔ $x+8$

4. *Multiple Choice*   What is the product $\dfrac{x^2 - 7x - 44}{x^2 + 6x - 16} \cdot \dfrac{x^2 + 17x + 72}{x^2 - 2x - 99}$?

Ⓐ $\dfrac{x \cdot + 9}{x - 2}$ Ⓑ $\dfrac{x-2}{x+4}$

Ⓒ $\dfrac{x+4}{x-2}$ Ⓓ $\dfrac{x-11}{x+9}$

Ⓔ $\dfrac{x+8}{x-2}$

Quantitative Comparison   **In Exercises 5 and 6, choose the statement below that is true about the given quantities.**

Ⓐ   The number in column A is greater.

Ⓑ   The number in column B is greater.

Ⓒ   The two numbers are equal.

Ⓓ   The relationship cannot be determined from the given information.

	Column A	Column B
5.	The coefficient a in the simplified form of $\dfrac{6x^2y}{7xy^4} \cdot \dfrac{14x^2y^3}{3xy}$; $\dfrac{ax^2}{by}$	The coefficient b in the simplified form of $\dfrac{6x^2y}{7xy^4} \cdot \dfrac{14x^2y^3}{3xy}$; $\dfrac{ax^2}{by}$
6.	The constant a in the product $\dfrac{x^2 + x - 12}{x^2 - 2x - 3} \cdot \dfrac{x^2 + 3x + 2}{x^2 + 12x + 32}$; $\dfrac{x+a}{x+b}$	The constant b in the product $\dfrac{x^2 + x - 12}{x^2 - 2x - 3} \cdot \dfrac{x^2 + 3x + 2}{x^2 + 12x + 32}$; $\dfrac{x+a}{x+b}$

Standardized Test Practice

For use with pages 562–567

TEST TAKING STRATEGY **Long-term preparation for a standardized test can be done throughout your high school career and can improve your overall abilities.**

1. **Multiple Choice** What is the sum $\dfrac{3x^2}{7x} + \dfrac{4x}{7x}$?

   (A) $\dfrac{7x^2}{7x}$

   (B) $\dfrac{3x^2 + 4x}{7x}$

   (C) $\dfrac{3x^2 + 4x}{7x^2}$

   (D) $\dfrac{3x^2 + 4x}{49x^2}$

   (E) $\dfrac{12x^3}{49x^2}$

2. **Multiple Choice** What is the sum $\dfrac{4}{3x^2} + \dfrac{x}{3x^2 - 6x}$?

   (A) $\dfrac{x^2 + 4}{3x^2(x - 2)}$

   (B) $\dfrac{x^2 + 4}{3x(x - 2)}$

   (C) $\dfrac{x^2 + 4x - 8}{3x^2(x - 2)}$

   (D) $\dfrac{x^2 + 4x - 8}{3x(x - 2)}$

   (E) $\dfrac{x^2 + 4x - 2}{3x^2(x - 2)}$

3. **Multiple Choice** What is the difference $\dfrac{x + 4}{x^2 + 6x + 9} - \dfrac{1}{x^2 - 9}$?

   (A) $\dfrac{x^2 - x - 15}{(x + 3)^2(x - 3)}$

   (B) $\dfrac{x^2 + x - 15}{(x + 3)^2(x - 3)}$

   (C) $\dfrac{x^2 - 15}{(x + 3)^2(x - 3)}$

   (D) $\dfrac{x^2 - 15}{(x - 3)^2(x + 3)}$

   (E) $\dfrac{x^2 + 15}{(x + 3)^2(x - 3)}$

4. **Multiple Choice** What is the simplified form of the following complex fraction?

   $$\dfrac{\dfrac{6}{x + 2}}{\dfrac{1}{4} + \dfrac{3}{x + 2}}$$

   (A) $\dfrac{24}{x + 3}$

   (B) $\dfrac{24}{x + 13}$

   (C) $\dfrac{6}{x + 5}$

   (D) $\dfrac{6}{4x + 11}$

   (E) $\dfrac{24}{x + 14}$

Quantitative Comparison **In Exercises 5 and 6, choose the statement below that is true about the given quantities.**

   (A) The number in column A is greater.

   (B) The number in column B is greater.

   (C) The two numbers are equal.

   (D) The relationship cannot be determined from the given information.

Column A	Column B
The constant a in the sum $\dfrac{2x}{5x^2} + \dfrac{3}{5x(x - 1)}$; $\dfrac{ax^2 + bx}{5x^2(x - 1)}$	The constant b in the sum $\dfrac{2x}{5x^2} + \dfrac{3}{5x(x - 1)}$; $\dfrac{ax^2 + bx}{5x^2(x - 1)}$
The constant a in the difference $\dfrac{x - 4}{x^2} - \dfrac{2}{x^3 - 2x^2}$; $\dfrac{x^2 - ax + b}{x^2(x - 2)}$	The constant b in the difference $\dfrac{x - 4}{x^2} - \dfrac{2}{x^3 - 2x^2}$; $\dfrac{x^2 - ax + b}{x^2(x - 2)}$

5.

6.

Standardized Test Practice

For use with pages 568–573

TEST TAKING STRATEGY If you find yourself spending too much time on one question and getting frustrated, move on to the next question.

1. *Multiple Choice* What is the solution of the equation $\dfrac{6}{x} - \dfrac{2}{3} = -\dfrac{4}{x}$?

   (A) 15   (B) -2 (C) -15

   (D) 3   (E) 6

2. *Multiple Choice* What is the solution of the equation $\dfrac{3}{x-1} = 4 + \dfrac{9}{x-1}$?

   (A) $-\dfrac{1}{2}$ (B) -1 (C) -2

   (D) 1   (E) $\dfrac{1}{2}$

3. *Multiple Choice* What is the solution of the equation $\dfrac{-5-x}{2} = -x + 1$?

   (A) 3   (B) -7 (C) -3

   (D) 1   (E) 7

4. *Multiple Choice* What are all the the solutions of the equation $\dfrac{-6}{x+7} = \dfrac{x}{2}$?

   (A) 3, 4   (B) $-3, 4$ (C) -4

   (D) -3 (E) $-4, -3$

Quantitative Comparison In Exercises 5–7, choose the statement below that is true about the given quantities.

   (A) The number in column A is greater.

   (B) The number in column B is greater.

   (C) The two numbers are equal.

   (D) The relationship cannot be determined from the given information.

	Column A	Column B
5.	The solution of $\dfrac{x}{8} - \dfrac{1}{6} = \dfrac{x-3}{3}$.	The solution of $\dfrac{x+6}{x-3} = -\dfrac{2}{7}$.
6.	The solution of $\dfrac{x-1}{x+2} = \dfrac{3}{4}$.	The solution of $\dfrac{3}{x} + \dfrac{2}{5} = \dfrac{7}{x}$.
7.	The solution of $\dfrac{-3+x}{8} = x - 10$.	The solution of $\dfrac{x+6}{3} = \dfrac{3x-6}{5}$.

8. *Multiple Choice* What are all the solutions of the equation $\dfrac{-5}{x-8} = \dfrac{x}{3}$?

   (A) $-5, -3$ (B) 3, 5   (C) $-3, 5$

   (D) $-5, 3$ (E) 3

9. *Multiple Choice* What are all the solutions of the equation $\dfrac{x+2}{5} = \dfrac{8}{x-4}$?

   (A) $-8, -6$ (B) 6, 8   (C) $-8, 6$

   (D) $-6, 8$ (E) 8

Algebra 2
Standardized Test Practice Workbook

Chapter 9

Standardized Test Practice

For use with pages 589–594

TEST TAKING STRATEGY   **The mathematical portion of a standardized test is based on concepts and skills taught in high school mathematics courses.**

1. *Multiple Choice*   What is the distance between $(-5, 2)$ and $(4, -8)$?

   (A) 6.08   (B) 13.45

   (C) 13.89   (D) 3.61

   (E) 10.37

2. *Multiple Choice*   What is the distance between $(10, -2)$ and $(-4, 6)$?

   (A) 6.38   (B) 7.21

   (C) 10.0   (D) 15.62

   (E) 16.12

3. *Multiple Choice*   What is the midpoint of the line segment connecting $(2, 7)$ and $(-8, 15)$?

   (A) $(3, 11)$ (B) $(-3, 11)$

   (C) $(3, -11)$ (D) $(11, 3)$

   (E) $(-11, -3)$

4. *Multiple Choice*   What is the midpoint of the line segment connecting $(-7, 4)$ and $(-3, 2)$?

   (A) $(-5, 3)$ (B) $(5, -3)$

   (C) $(3, 5)$ (D) $(-3, -5)$

   (E) $(-5, -3)$

5. *Multiple Choice*   Which equation represents the perpendicular bisector of the line segment connecting $(-7, 5)$ and $(2, -4)$?

   (A) $y = -x - 1$ (B) $y = -x - 3$

   (C) $y = x + 3$ (D) $y = x - 3$

   (E) $y = -x + 3$

6. *Multiple Choice*   Which equation represents the perpendicular bisector of the line segment connecting $(3, -1)$ and $(-9, 5)$?

   (A) $y = -2x + 8$ (B) $y = 2x - 8$

   (C) $y = -2x - 4$ (D) $y = 2x + 8$

   (E) $y = 2x - 4$

Quantitative Comparison   **In Exercises 7–9, choose the statement below that is true about the given quantities.**

   (A)   The number in column A is greater.

   (B)   The number in column B is greater.

   (C)   The two numbers are equal.

   (D)   The relationship cannot be determined from the given information.

	Column A	Column B
7.	Distance between $(4, 1)$ and $(-3, 0)$	Distance between $(6, -2)$ and $(-3, -8)$
8.	Distance between $(2, -5)$ and $(1, 7)$	Distance between $(-11, 1)$ and $(4, 6)$
9.	Distance between $(-9, 1)$ and $(10, 4)$	Distance between $(1, 9)$ and $(4, -10)$

NAME _____ DATE _____

Standardized Test Practice

For use with pages 595–600

TEST TAKING STRATEGY **During a test, draw graphs and figures in your test booklet to help you solve problems.**

1. *Multiple Choice* What is the focus of the parabola with equation $16y = x^2$?

   Ⓐ (4, 0)   Ⓑ (16, 0)

   Ⓒ (0, 16)   Ⓓ (0, −4)

   Ⓔ (0, 4)

2. *Multiple Choice* What is the focus of the parabola with equation $2y^2 = 8x$?

   Ⓐ (1, 0)   Ⓑ (0, 1)

   Ⓒ (−1, 0)   Ⓓ (0, 2)

   Ⓔ (4, 0)

3. *Multiple Choice* What is the directrix of the parabola with equation $x^2 = -28y$?

   Ⓐ $x = 28$ Ⓑ $y = -7$

   Ⓒ $y = 7$ Ⓓ $y = -28$

   Ⓔ $x = 7$

4. *Multiple Choice* What is the directrix of the parabola with equation $36x = 9y^2$?

   Ⓐ $x = 1$ Ⓑ $x = -1$

   Ⓒ $y = 4$ Ⓓ $y = -4$

   Ⓔ $x = -4$

5. *Multiple Choice* What is the directrix of the parabola with equation $5x^2 = -40y$?

   Ⓐ $x = 2$ Ⓑ $y = -8$

   Ⓒ $y = 8$ Ⓓ $y = 2$

   Ⓔ $x = -2$

6. *Multiple Choice* Which equation is graphed?

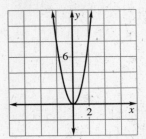

   Ⓐ $x^2 = -\dfrac{1}{2}y$ Ⓑ $y^2 = 2x$

   Ⓒ $x^2 = \dfrac{1}{2}y$ Ⓓ $y^2 = -\dfrac{1}{2}x$

   Ⓔ $x^2 = 2y$

7. *Multi-Step Problem* The cross section of a television antenna dish is a parabola and the receiver is located at the focus.

   a. If the receiver is located 5 feet above the vertex (assume the vertex is at the origin), find an equation for the cross section of the dish.

   b. If the dish is 10 feet wide, how deep is it?

   c. *Critical Thinking* If another television antenna dish is available that is 2.5 feet deep with the same width as in part (b), where is the receiver located?

LESSON 10.3

Standardized Test Practice

NAME _____ DATE _____

For use with pages 601–607

TEST TAKING STRATEGY If the answers to a question are formulas, substitute the given numbers into the formulas to test the possible answers.

1. *Multiple Choice* Which equation is graphed?

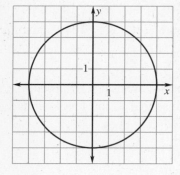

Ⓐ $x^2 - y^2 = 16$ Ⓑ $x^2 + y^2 = 16$
Ⓒ $x^2 + y^2 = 4$ Ⓓ $x^2 - y^2 = 4$
Ⓔ $2x^2 + 2y^2 = 8$

2. *Multiple Choice* Which is the standard form of the equation where the point $(-2, 4)$ is on a circle whose center is the origin?
Ⓐ $x^2 - y^2 = 20$ Ⓑ $x^2 + y^2 = 8$
Ⓒ $x^2 + y^2 = 20$ Ⓓ $x^2 - y^2 = 8$
Ⓔ $5x^2 + 5y^2 = 25$

3. *Multiple Choice* Which is the standard form of the equation where the point $(3, -6)$ is on a circle whose center is the origin?
Ⓐ $x^2 + y^2 = 45$ Ⓑ $x^2 + y^2 = 3$
Ⓒ $3x^2 + 3y^2 = 120$ Ⓓ $x^2 - y^2 = 6$
Ⓔ $2x^2 - 2y^2 = 90$

4. *Multiple Choice* What is the equation of the line that is tangent to the circle $x^2 + y^2 = 25$ at the point $(4, 3)$?
Ⓐ $y = \frac{4}{3}x + \frac{25}{3}$ Ⓑ $y = \frac{4}{3}x$
Ⓒ $y = -\frac{3}{4}x + 6$ Ⓓ $y = -\frac{4}{3}x - \frac{25}{3}$
Ⓔ $y = -\frac{4}{3}x + \frac{25}{3}$

5. *Multiple Choice* Suppose a signal from a radio transmitter tower can be received up to 175 miles away. The following points represent the locations of houses near the transmitter tower with the origin representing the tower. Which point is *not* within the range of the tower?
Ⓐ (40, 120) Ⓑ (60, 125)
Ⓒ (85, 100) Ⓓ (55, 185)
Ⓔ (90, 150)

Quantitative Comparison In Exercises 6–8, choose the statement below that is true about the given quantities.
Ⓐ The number in column A is greater.
Ⓑ The number in column B is greater.
Ⓒ The two numbers are equal.
Ⓓ The relationship cannot be determined from the given information.

	Column A	Column B
6.	The length of the radius of a circle with equation $x^2 + y^2 = 12$	The length of the radius of a circle with equation $4x^2 + 4y^2 = 48$
7.	The length of the radius of a circle with equation $2x^2 + 2y^2 = 18$	The length of the radius of a circle with equation $x^2 + y^2 = 16$
8.	The length of the radius of a circle with equation $x^2 + y^2 = 52$	The length of the radius of a circle with equation $3x^2 + 3y^2 = 153$

Standardized Test Practice

For use with pages 609–614

TEST TAKING STRATEGY   **When checking your answer to a question, try using a method different from one you used to get the answer.**

1. *Multiple Choice* What are the foci of the ellipse $8x^2 + 12y^2 = 96$?

   Ⓐ $(-2, 0), (2, 0)$ Ⓑ $(0, -2), (0, 2)$

   Ⓒ $(0, -3), (0, 3)$ Ⓓ $(-3, 0), (3, 0)$

   Ⓔ $(-2, 0), (0, 2)$

2. *Multiple Choice* What are the foci of the ellipse $17x^2 + 8y^2 = 136$?

   Ⓐ $(-5, 0), (5, 0)$ Ⓑ $(0, -5), (0, 5)$

   Ⓒ $(0, -3), (0, 3)$ Ⓓ $(-3, 0), (3, 0)$

   Ⓔ $(-5, 0), (0, 5)$

3. *Multiple Choice* What is the equation of the ellipse with center at $(0, 0)$, vertex at $(0, 3)$, and co-vertex at $(-2, 0)$?

   Ⓐ $\dfrac{x^2}{9} + \dfrac{y^2}{4} = 1$ Ⓑ $\dfrac{x^2}{2} + \dfrac{y^2}{3} = 1$

   Ⓒ $\dfrac{x^2}{4} + \dfrac{y^2}{9} = 1$ Ⓓ $\dfrac{x^2}{3} + \dfrac{y^2}{2} = 1$

   Ⓔ $\dfrac{y^2}{3} - \dfrac{x^2}{2} = 1$

4. *Multiple Choice* What is the equation of the ellipse with center at $(0, 0)$, vertex at $(5, 0)$, and focus at $(3, 0)$?

   Ⓐ $\dfrac{x^2}{5} + \dfrac{y^2}{3} = 1$ Ⓑ $\dfrac{x^2}{25} + \dfrac{y^2}{9} = 1$

   Ⓒ $\dfrac{x^2}{9} + \dfrac{y^2}{25} = 1$ Ⓓ $\dfrac{x^2}{25} + \dfrac{y^2}{21} = 1$

   Ⓔ $\dfrac{x^2}{21} + \dfrac{y^2}{25} = 1$

5. *Multiple Choice* What is the approximate area of an ellipse that is 150 feet long and 25 feet wide?

   Ⓐ 6300 square feet   Ⓑ 3000 square feet

   Ⓒ 2100 square feet   Ⓓ 1000 square feet

   Ⓔ 1500 square feet

6. *Multiple Choice* What is the approximate area of an ellipse that is 250 feet long and 80 feet wide?

   Ⓐ 63,000 square feet

   Ⓑ 31,000 square feet

   Ⓒ 42,000 square feet

   Ⓓ 28,000 square feet

   Ⓔ 16,000 square feet

7. *Multi-Step Problem* You are constructing an elliptical flower garden that is to be 16 feet long and 8 feet wide.

   a. Write an equation for the garden assuming that the major axis of the garden is horizontal.

   b. Graph the equation.

   c. Label the vertices, co-vertices, and foci.

   d. Determine the approximate area of the garden.

   e. *Critical Thinking* Explain what happens to the area of the garden if you increase the length by 2 feet and shorten the width by 2 feet.

Standardized Test Practice

For use with pages 615–621

TEST TAKING STRATEGY   **If you get stuck on a question, select an answer choice and check to see if it is a reasonable answer to the question.**

1. *Multiple Choice*   Which equation is graphed?

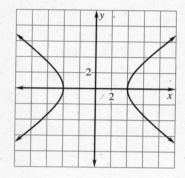

  Ⓐ $9y^2 - 16x^2 = 144$

  Ⓑ $9x^2 + 16y^2 = 144$

  Ⓒ $16y^2 - 9x^2 = 144$

  Ⓓ $9x^2 - 16y^2 = 144$

  Ⓔ None of these

2. *Multiple Choice*   Which equation is graphed?

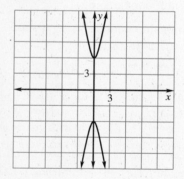

  Ⓐ $y^2 - 36x^2 = 36$

  Ⓑ $36x^2 - y^2 = 36$

  Ⓒ $36y^2 - x^2 = 36$

  Ⓓ $x^2 - 36y^2 = 36$

  Ⓔ None of these

3. *Multiple Choice*   What is the standard form of the hyperbola with foci at $(0, \pm 5)$ and vertices at $(0, \pm 2)$?

  Ⓐ $\dfrac{y^2}{21} - \dfrac{x^2}{4} = 1$ Ⓑ $\dfrac{x^2}{21} - \dfrac{y^2}{4} = 1$

  Ⓒ $\dfrac{y^2}{4} - \dfrac{x^2}{21} = 1$ Ⓓ $\dfrac{x^2}{4} - \dfrac{y^2}{21} = 1$

  Ⓔ None of these

4. *Multiple Choice*   What is the standard form of the hyperbola with foci at $(\pm 4, 0)$ and vertices at $(\pm 3, 0)$?

  Ⓐ $\dfrac{y^2}{9} - \dfrac{x^2}{7} = 1$ Ⓑ $\dfrac{x^2}{7} - \dfrac{y^2}{9} = 1$

  Ⓒ $\dfrac{y^2}{7} - \dfrac{x^2}{9} = 1$ Ⓓ $\dfrac{x^2}{9} - \dfrac{y^2}{7} = 1$

  Ⓔ None of these

5. *Multi-Step Problem*   A hyperbolic mirror can be used to take panoramic photographs. A camera is pointed toward the vertex of the mirror and is positioned so that the lens is at one focus of the mirror.

  a. Suppose a mirror has a cross section modeled by the equation

$$\frac{y^2}{4} - \frac{x^2}{25} = 1$$

    where x and y are measured in inches. How far from the mirror is the lens?

  b. Suppose a mirror has a cross section modeled by the equation

$$\frac{x^2}{8} - \frac{y^2}{12} = 1$$

    where x and y are measured in inches. How far is the lens from the vertex of the mirror?

  c. *Critical Thinking*   Find an equation for the cross section of the mirror if the lens is 8 inches from the vertex of the mirror and the lens is positioned at the focus $(0, -6)$.

Standardized Test Practice

For use with pages 623–631

During the test, do not worry excessively about how much time you have left. Concentrate on the question in front of you.

1. *Multiple Choice*   Which of the following is an equation of the parabola whose vertex is at $(4, -3)$ and whose focus is at $(4, 8)$?

   (A) $(x - 3)^2 = 44(y - 4)$

   (B) $(x - 4)^2 = 44(y + 3)$

   (C) $(y - 4)^2 = 44(x - 3)$

   (D) $(x + 3)^2 = 44(y + 4)$

   (E) $(y - 4)^2 = 44(x + 3)$

2. *Multiple Choice*   Which of the following is an equation of the circle whose center is at $(-3, 6)$ and the radius is 4?

   (A) $(x - 3)^2 + (y - 6)^2 = 16$

   (B) $(x + 3)^2 + (y + 6)^2 = 16$

   (C) $(x + 3)^2 - (y - 6)^2 = 16$

   (D) $(x + 3)^2 + (y - 6)^2 = 16$

   (E) $(x - 3)^2 - (y - 6)^2 = 16$

3. *Multiple Choice*   Which of the following is an equation of the ellipse with foci at $(2, 4)$ and $(-6, 4)$ and vertices at $(-8, 4)$ and $(4, 4)$?

   (A) $\dfrac{(x + 4)^2}{20} + \dfrac{(y - 2)^2}{36} = 1$

   (B) $\dfrac{(x + 4)^2}{36} + \dfrac{(y - 2)^2}{20} = 1$

   (C) $\dfrac{(x + 2)^2}{36} + \dfrac{(y - 4)^2}{20} = 1$

   (D) $\dfrac{(x + 2)^2}{20} + \dfrac{(y - 4)^2}{36} = 1$

   (E) $\dfrac{(x - 2)^2}{36} + \dfrac{(y + 4)^2}{20} = 1$

4. *Multiple Choice*   What conic does the equation $y^2 - x^2 - 6y - 12x - 28 = 0$ represent?

   (A) parabola   (B) circle

   (C) ellipse   (D) hyperbola

   (E) None of these

5. *Multiple Choice*   What conic does the equation $x^2 + y^2 - 4x + 6y + 9 = 0$ represent?

   (A) parabola   (B) circle

   (C) ellipse   (D) hyperbola

   (E) None of these

Quantitative Comparison   **In Exercises 6–8, choose the statement below that is true about the given quantities.**

   (A) The number in column A is greater.

   (B) The number in column B is greater.

   (C) The two numbers are equal.

   (D) The relationship cannot be determined from the given information.

	Column A	Column B
6.	h in the standard form of the equation of a circle with center at $(6, -4)$ and radius is 3	k in the standard form of the equation of a circle with center at $(6, -4)$ and radius is 3
7.	h in the standard form of the equation of a parabola with vertex at $(-2, 3)$ and focus at $(-2, 6)$	k in the standard form of the equation of a parabola with vertex at $(-2, 3)$ and focus at $(-2, 6)$
8.	h in the standard form of the equation of a hyperbola with vertices at $(1, -8)$ and $(1, 10)$	k in the standard form of the equation of a hyperbola with vertices at $(1, -8)$ and $(1, 10)$

NAME _____ DATE _____

Standardized Test Practice

For use with pages 632–638

TEST TAKING STRATEGY   **When taking a test, go back and answer questions that you suspect will take you extra time and effort.**

1. *Multiple Choice*   What point is the intersection of the graphs of $x^2 + y^2 = 25$ and $y = x + 7$?

  Ⓐ $(3, 4)$ Ⓑ $(-3, 4)$

  Ⓒ $(4, 3)$ Ⓓ $(-4, -3)$

  Ⓔ $(-3, -4)$

2. *Multiple Choice*   What point is the intersection of the graphs of $x^2 - 4y = 13$ and $x^2 + y^2 = 34$?

  Ⓐ $(5, 3)$ Ⓑ $(-5, -3)$

  Ⓒ $(3, 5)$ Ⓓ $(-3, -5)$

  Ⓔ $(5, -3)$

3. *Multiple Choice*   What point is the intersection of the graphs of $x^2 - y^2 = 5$ and $2x^2 + y^2 = 22$?

  Ⓐ $(2, 3)$ Ⓑ $(-2, -3)$

  Ⓒ $(5, 0)$ Ⓓ $(0, -5)$

  Ⓔ $(3, -2)$

4. *Multiple Choice*   What point is the intersection of the graphs of $x = -y$, $x^2 + y = 2$, and $-y^2 + 3x = 2$?

  Ⓐ $(2, 2)$ Ⓑ $(-2, -2)$

  Ⓒ $(2, 0)$ Ⓓ $(-2, 2)$

  Ⓔ $(2, -2)$

5. *Multiple Choice*   What point is the intersection of the graphs of $y = 3x$, $x^2 + 4y^2 = 37$ and $y^2 - x^2 = 8$?

  Ⓐ $(3, 1)$ Ⓑ $(-1, 3)$

  Ⓒ $(-1, -3)$ Ⓓ $(-3, 1)$

  Ⓔ $(1, -3)$

Quantitative Comparison   **In Exercises 6–8, choose the statement below that is true about the given quantities.**

  Ⓐ The number in column A is greater.

  Ⓑ The number in column B is greater.

  Ⓒ The two numbers are equal.

  Ⓓ The relationship cannot be determined from the given information.

	Column A	*Column B*
6.	The number of points of intersection of the graphs of $x^2 + y^2 = 1$ and $3x^2 + 5y^2 = 15$	The number of points of intersection of the graphs of $x^2 + y^2 = 4$ and $y = x - 2$
7.	The number of points of intersection of the graphs of $y - 2x = 0$ and $x^2 - 2x - 3 = 4$	The number of points of intersection of the graphs of $y = 2x + 1$ and $y = (x + 1)^2$
8.	The number of points of intersection of the graphs of $x^2 - 2y^2 = 25$ and $x^2 + y^2 = 25$	The number of points of intersection of the graphs of $x^2 + y^2 = 16$ and $x^2 + 4y^2 = 36$

TEST TAKING STRATEGY   **If you start to get tense during a test, put your pencil down and take some deep breaths. This may help you regain control.**

1. **Multiple Choice**   What is the third term of the sequence defined by $a_n = 4n + 6$?

   Ⓐ 6   Ⓑ 10
   Ⓒ 14   Ⓓ 18
   Ⓔ 22

2. **Multiple Choice**   What is the fifth term of the sequence defined by $a_n = 3n - 1$?

   Ⓐ 2   Ⓑ 8
   Ⓒ 14   Ⓓ 20
   Ⓔ 26

3. **Multiple Choice**   What is the next term in the sequence 1, 6, 11, 16, 21, . . . ?

   Ⓐ 23   Ⓑ 26
   Ⓒ 28   Ⓓ 30
   Ⓔ 32

4. **Multiple Choice**   What is the next term in the sequence 4, 7, 10, 13, 16, . . . ?

   Ⓐ 19   Ⓑ 21
   Ⓒ 23   Ⓓ 25
   Ⓔ 27

5. **Multiple Choice**   Which series is represented by

   $$\sum_{i=1}^{3} (5i + 3)?$$

   Ⓐ 8 + 13 + 18 + · · ·
   Ⓑ 3 + 8 + 13
   Ⓒ 13 + 18 + 23
   Ⓓ 8 + 11 + 14
   Ⓔ 8 + 13 + 18

6. **Multiple Choice**   Which series is represented by

   $$\sum_{k=2}^{4} (2k^2 + k)?$$

   Ⓐ 3 + 10 + 21   Ⓑ 10 + 21 + 36
   Ⓒ 3 + 7 + 11   Ⓓ 10 + 14 + 18
   Ⓔ 10 + 21 + 32

Quantitative Comparison   **In Exercises 7–10, choose the statement below that is true about the given quantities.**

   Ⓐ   The number in column A is greater.

   Ⓑ   The number in column B is greater.

   Ⓒ   The two numbers are equal.

   Ⓓ   The relationship cannot be determined from the given information.

	Column A	Column B
7.	The seventh term of the sequence defined by $a_n = 4n + 13$	The seventh term of the sequence defined by $a_n = 6n - 1$
8.	$\sum_{n=1}^{6} (3 - n)$	$\sum_{n=1}^{6} (n - 3)$
9.	$\sum_{k=2}^{4} (k^2 - 5)$	$\sum_{k=1}^{3} (k^2 + 2k - 4)$
10.	The fourth term of the sequence defined by $a_n = n^2 + 1$	The sixth term of the sequence defined by $a_n = 3n - 2$

Standardized Test Practice

For use with pages 659–665

TEST TAKING STRATEGY **Even though you must keep your answer sheet neat, you can make any kind of mark you want in your test booklet.**

1. *Multiple Choice* Which of the following is an arithmetic sequence?

Ⓐ $2, 5, 9, 14, 20, \ldots$

Ⓑ $1, 3, 6, 10, 15, \ldots$

Ⓒ $-5, -2, 1, 4, 7, \ldots$

Ⓓ $-3, 0, 4, 9, 15, \ldots$

Ⓔ $3, 5, 8, 12, 17, \ldots$

2. *Multiple Choice* Which of the following is an arithmetic sequence?

Ⓐ $2, 4, 8, 14, 22, \ldots$

Ⓑ $1, 5, 6, 10, 11, \ldots$

Ⓒ $3, 9, 21, 39, 63, \ldots$

Ⓓ $-3, 0, 6, 15, 27, \ldots$

Ⓔ $3, 8, 13, 18, 23, \ldots$

3. *Multiple Choice* What is a rule for the nth term of the arithmetic sequence with $a_{10} = 22$ and common difference $d = 3$?

Ⓐ $a_n = 3n - 2$ Ⓑ $a_n = 3n - 8$

Ⓒ $a_n = 3n + 4$ Ⓓ $a_n = 3n - 6$

Ⓔ $a_n = 3n + 5$

4. *Multiple Choice* What is a rule for the nth term of the arithmetic sequence with $a_{21} = 147$ and common difference $d = 11$?

Ⓐ $a_n = 11n - 21$ Ⓑ $a_n = 11n - 42$

Ⓒ $a_n = 11n + 21$ Ⓓ $a_n = 11n + 32$

Ⓔ $a_n = 11n - 84$

5. *Multiple Choice* What is a rule for the nth term of the arithmetic sequence with $a_8 = 21$ and $a_{14} = 45$?

Ⓐ $a_n = 4n - 11$ Ⓑ $a_n = 4n - 8$

Ⓒ $a_n = 4n + 1$ Ⓓ $a_n = 4n + 7$

Ⓔ $a_n = 4n + 11$

6. *Multiple Choice* What is the sum of the first 20 terms of the series

$$3 + 14 + 25 + 36 + \cdots ?$$

Ⓐ 226   Ⓑ 1252

Ⓒ 1860   Ⓓ 2010

Ⓔ 2150

Quantitative Comparison **In Exercises 7–9, choose the statement below that is true about the given quantities.**

Ⓐ The number in column A is greater.

Ⓑ The number in column B is greater.

Ⓒ The two numbers are equal.

Ⓓ The relationship cannot be determined from the given information.

	Column A	Column B
7.	The sum of the first 10 terms of the series $6 + 9 + 12 + 15 + \cdots$	The sum of the first 15 terms of the series $2 + 5 + 8 + 11 + \cdots$
8.	The value of n for which $a_n = 43$ when $a_4 = 8$ and $a_{18} = 106$	The value of n for which $a_n = 37$ when $a_3 = 13$ and $a_{22} = 89$
9.	The value of a_{13} when $a_2 = 5$ and $a_{21} = 62$	The value of a_{20} when $a_4 = 2$ and $a_{25} = 44$

Standardized Test Practice

TEST TAKING STRATEGY   **If you use the same method to find and check an answer, you may make the same mistake twice.**

1. *Multiple Choice* Which of the following is a geometric sequence?

- Ⓐ $1, 2, 3, 4, 5, \ldots$
- Ⓑ $1, 3, 9, 27, 81, \ldots$
- Ⓒ $7, 12, 17, 22, 27, \ldots$
- Ⓓ $-4, 0, 4, 8, 12, \ldots$
- Ⓔ $-6, -4, -2, 0, 2, \ldots$

2. *Multiple Choice* Which of the following is a geometric sequence?

- Ⓐ $1, 2, 4, 8, 16, \ldots$
- Ⓑ $-3, 1, 5, 9, \ldots$
- Ⓒ $4, 8, 24, 96, 480, \ldots$
- Ⓓ $-5, 0, 10, 25, 45, \ldots$
- Ⓔ $-2, -4, 8, 16, -32, \ldots$

3. *Multiple Choice* What is a rule for the *n*th term of the geometric sequence $-3, -6, -12, -24, -48, \ldots$?

- Ⓐ $a_n = 2(-3)^{n-1}$
- Ⓑ $a_n = -3(2)^{n-1}$
- Ⓒ $a_n = 3(-2)^{n-1}$
- Ⓓ $a_n = -3(-2)^{n-1}$
- Ⓔ $a_n = -2(3)^{n-1}$

4. *Multiple Choice* What is a rule for the *n*th term of the geometric sequence with $a_4 = -18$ and common ratio $r = 2$?

- Ⓐ $a_n = 2.25(2)^{n-1}$
- Ⓑ $a_n = 2(2.25)^{n-1}$
- Ⓒ $a_n = -2(2.25)^{n-1}$
- Ⓓ $a_n = -2.25(2)^{n-1}$
- Ⓔ $a_n = -2.25(-2)^{n-1}$

5. *Multiple Choice* What is a rule for the *n*th term of the geometric sequence with $a_2 = 4$ and $a_6 = 2500$?

- Ⓐ $a_n = 0.8(5)^{n-1}$
- Ⓑ $a_n = 4(5)^{n-1}$
- Ⓒ $a_n = -0.8(5)^{n-1}$
- Ⓓ $a_n = -4(5)^{n-1}$
- Ⓔ $a_n = 5(0.8)^{n-1}$

6. *Multiple Choice* What is the sum of the first 12 terms of the geometric series $1 + 2 + 4 + 8 + 16 + \cdots$?

- Ⓐ 240
- Ⓑ 880
- Ⓒ 1060
- Ⓓ 1850
- Ⓔ 4095

7. *Multi-Step Problem* Suppose two computer companies, Company A and Company B, opened in 1991. The revenues of Company A increased arithmetically through 2000, while the revenues of Company B increased geometrically through 2000. In 1995 the revenue of Company A was $316.3 million. In 1995 the revenue of Company B was $35.2 million.

a. The revenues of Company A have a common difference of 43.1. The revenues of Company B have a common ratio of 2. Find a rule for the revenues in the *n*th year of each company. Let a_1 represent 1991.

b. Graph each sequence from part (a).

c. Find the sum of the revenues from 1991 through 2000 for each company.

d. *Writing* Use a graphing calculator or spreadsheet to find when the revenue of Company B is greater than the revenue of Company A. Explain which company you would rather own referring to the graphs from part (b).

Standardized Test Practice

For use with pages 675–680

TEST TAKING STRATEGY   Draw an arrow on your test booklet next to questions that you do not answer. This will enable you to find the questions quickly when you go back.

1. *Multiple Choice*   What is the sum of the series

$$1 - \frac{1}{3} + \frac{1}{9} - \frac{1}{27} + \cdots ?$$

Ⓐ $\frac{3}{4}$ Ⓑ $\frac{2}{3}$ Ⓒ $\frac{7}{8}$

Ⓓ $\frac{5}{6}$ Ⓔ $\frac{4}{9}$

2. *Multiple Choice*   What is the sum of the series

$$\sum_{i=1}^{\infty} 3(0.2)^{i-1}?$$

Ⓐ 2.25   Ⓑ 2.75   Ⓒ 3.25

Ⓓ 3.75   Ⓔ 4.25

3. *Multiple Choice*   What is the common ratio of an infinite geometric series whose sum is 30 and the first term is $a_1 = 6$?

Ⓐ $\frac{2}{3}$ Ⓑ $\frac{1}{5}$ Ⓒ $\frac{3}{4}$

Ⓓ $\frac{4}{5}$ Ⓔ $\frac{4}{7}$

4. *Multiple Choice*   What is the common ratio of an infinite geometric series whose sum is 125 and the first term is $a_1 = 625$?

Ⓐ $-\frac{1}{2}$ Ⓑ 2   Ⓒ -2

Ⓓ 4   Ⓔ -4

5. *Multiple Choice*   What fraction is equivalent to the repeating decimal 4.54545 . . . ?

Ⓐ $\frac{29}{7}$ Ⓑ $\frac{50}{11}$ Ⓒ $\frac{75}{17}$

Ⓓ $\frac{81}{19}$ Ⓔ $\frac{125}{26}$

6. *Multiple Choice*   A ball is dropped from a height of 7 feet. Each time it hits the ground, it bounces half of its previous height. What is the total distance traveled by the ball?

Ⓐ   7 feet   Ⓑ   14 feet

Ⓒ   21 feet   Ⓓ   28 feet

Ⓔ   35 feet

Quantitative Comparison   **In Exercises 7 and 8, choose the statement below that is true about the given quantities.**

Ⓐ   The number in column A is greater.

Ⓑ   The number in column B is greater.

Ⓒ   The two numbers are equal.

Ⓓ   The relationship cannot be determined from the given information.

	Column A	Column B
7.	$\sum_{i=1}^{\infty} 3(-0.1)^{i-1}$	$\sum_{i=1}^{\infty} 5(-0.2)^{i-1}$
8.	$\sum_{i=1}^{\infty} \frac{1}{2}\left(\frac{2}{5}\right)^{i-1}$	$\sum_{i=1}^{\infty} \frac{3}{4}\left(-\frac{1}{3}\right)^{i-1}$

Standardized Test Practice

For use with pages 681–688

TEST TAKING STRATEGY   **During a test it is important to stay mentally focused, but also physically relaxed.**

1. *Multiple Choice*   What is the fifth term of the sequence whose first term is $a_1 = 8$ and whose nth term is $a_n = 3a_{n-1} + 7$?

  Ⓐ   31   Ⓑ   100   Ⓒ   307

  Ⓓ   928   Ⓔ   2791

2. *Multiple Choice*   What is the fourth term of the sequence whose first term is $a_1 = 2$ and whose nth term is $a_n = 4a_{n-1} - 11$?

  Ⓐ -3 Ⓑ -23 Ⓒ -103

  Ⓓ -423 Ⓔ -1703

3. *Multiple Choice*   What is a recursive rule for the arithmetic sequence with $a_1 = -3$ and $d = 8$?

  Ⓐ $a_1 = -3, a_n = 8n - 11$

  Ⓑ $a_1 = -3, a_n = 8n + 3$

  Ⓒ $a_1 = -3, a_n = a_{n-1} - 8$

  Ⓓ $a_1 = -3, a_n = a_{n-1} + 3$

  Ⓔ $a_1 = -3, a_n = a_{n-1} + 8$

4. *Multiple Choice*   What is a recursive rule for the geometric sequence with $a_1 = 4$ and $r = 0.2$?

  Ⓐ $a_1 = 4, a_n = 4(0.2)^{n-1}$

  Ⓑ $a_1 = 4, a_n = a_{n-1} + 0.2$

  Ⓒ $a_1 = 4, a_n = 4a_{n-1} + 0.2$

  Ⓓ $a_1 = 4, a_n = (0.2)a_{n-1}$

  Ⓔ $a_1 = 4, a_{n-1} = (0.2)a_n$

5. *Multiple Choice*   What is a recursive rule for the sequence 3, 12, 48, 192, . . . ?

  Ⓐ $a_n = 3(4)^{n-1}$

  Ⓑ $a_1 = 3, a_n = 3a_{n-1} + 4$

  Ⓒ $a_1 = 3, a_n = 4a_{n-1}$

  Ⓓ $a_n = 4(3)^{n-1}$

  Ⓔ $a_1 = 4, a_n = 3a_{n-1}$

6. *Multiple Choice*   What is a recursive rule for the sequence 5, -6.5, 8.45, -10.985, . . . ?

  Ⓐ $a_1 = 5, a_n = (-1.5)a_{n-1}$

  Ⓑ $a_1 = 5, a_n = (1.5)a_{n-1}$

  Ⓒ $a_n = 5(-1.3)a_{n-1}$

  Ⓓ $a_1 = 5, a_n = (-1.3)a_{n-1}$

  Ⓔ $a_1 = 5, a_n = (1.3)a_{n-1}$

7. *Multi-Step Problem*   Suppose a tree farm initially has 4000 pine trees. Each year 20% of the trees are harvested and 400 new seedlings are planted.

  a. Write a recursive rule for the number of pine trees on the tree farm after n years.

  b. Use the recursive rule from part (a) to determine the number of pine trees remaining after 4 years.

  c. Graph the sequence from part (a) over a period of ten years.

  d. *Critical Thinking*   Explain using the graph from part (c) what you would expect to happen over an extended period of time.

Chapter 11

Standardized Test Practice

For use with pages 701–707

TEST TAKING STRATEGY **Long-term preparation for a standardized test can be done throughout your high school career and can improve your overall abilities.**

1. *Multiple Choice* In how many ways can 10 runners finish a race first, second, or third?

　Ⓐ 3　　Ⓑ 10　　Ⓒ 300

　Ⓓ 720　　Ⓔ 1000

2. *Multiple Choice* In an activity club with 30 students, the offices of president, vice president, and treasurer will be filled. In how many ways can the offices be filled?

　Ⓐ 30　　Ⓑ 90　　Ⓒ 150

　Ⓓ 27,000　　Ⓔ 24,360

3. *Multiple Choice* How many different license plates are possible if two digits are followed by three letters?

　Ⓐ 98　　Ⓑ 876,450

　Ⓒ 1,404,000　　Ⓓ 1,757,600

　Ⓔ 12,647,200

4. *Multiple Choice* How many distinguishable permutations of the letters in BANANA are there?

　Ⓐ 60　　Ⓑ 120　　Ⓒ 180

　Ⓓ 360　　Ⓔ 720

5. *Multiple Choice* How many distinguishable permutations of the letters in BALLOON are there?

　Ⓐ 210　　Ⓑ 340　　Ⓒ 1260

　Ⓓ 2880　　Ⓔ 5040

Quantitative Comparison **In Exercises 6–8, choose the statement below that is true about the given quantities.**

　Ⓐ The number in column A is greater.

　Ⓑ The number in column B is greater.

　Ⓒ The two numbers are equal.

　Ⓓ The relationship cannot be determined from the given information.

	Column A	Column B
6.	$_8P_4$	$_{10}P_2$
7.	The number of permutations of 14 objects taken 2 at a time	The number of permutations of 7 objects taken 6 at a time
8.	6!	$_6P_5$

9. *Multiple Choice* How many different license plates are possible if three digits are followed by two letters?

　Ⓐ 1560　　Ⓑ 676,000

　Ⓒ 1,320,000　　Ⓓ 1,845,300

　Ⓔ 2,225,200

10. *Multiple Choice* In how many ways can 8 runners finish a race first, second, or third?

　Ⓐ 3　　Ⓑ 8　　Ⓒ 24

　Ⓓ 336　　Ⓔ 512

Chapter 12

Standardized Test Practice

For use with pages 708–715

TEST TAKING STRATEGY   **When taking a test, first tackle the questions that you know are easy for you to answer.**

1. *Multiple Choice*   In how many ways can 3 cards be chosen from a standard deck of 52 cards?

   Ⓐ 156   Ⓑ 2210

   Ⓒ 10,850   Ⓓ 22,100

   Ⓔ 132,600

2. *Multiple Choice*   In how many ways can a 7 person committee be chosen from a group of 10 people?

   Ⓐ 120   Ⓑ 1260

   Ⓒ 12,600   Ⓓ 60,480

   Ⓔ 604,800

3. *Multiple Choice*   A movie theater has 14 different movies showing. If you want to attend no more than 3 of the movies, how many different combinations of movies can you attend?

   Ⓐ 142   Ⓑ 364

   Ⓒ 470   Ⓓ 15,915

   Ⓔ 16,387

4. *Multiple Choice*   What is the coefficient of x^4 in the expansion of $(3x + 1)^7$?

   Ⓐ 35   Ⓑ 105   Ⓒ 315

   Ⓓ 945   Ⓔ 2835

5. *Multiple Choice*   What is the coefficient of x^3 in the expansion of $(2x - 3)^5$?

   Ⓐ 80   Ⓑ 720

   Ⓒ −120   Ⓓ −360

   Ⓔ 360

6. *Multi-Step Problem*   You are buying a flower arrangement. The florist has 15 types of flowers and 8 types of vases.

   a. If you can afford exactly 4 types of flowers and need only 1 vase, how many different arrangements can you buy?

   b. If you can afford exactly 11 types of flowers and need 7 vases, how many different arrangements can you buy?

   c. *Critical Thinking*   Compare the solutions to parts (a) and (b).

7. *Multiple Choice*   In how many ways can 50 cards be chosen from a standard deck of 52 cards?

   Ⓐ 1326   Ⓑ 6540

   Ⓒ 16,445   Ⓓ 32,872

   Ⓔ 212,961

8. *Multiple Choice*   An amusement park has 27 different rides. If you have 21 ride tickets, how many different combinations of rides can you take?

   Ⓐ 567   Ⓑ 2320

   Ⓒ 6740   Ⓓ 112,480

   Ⓔ 296,010

9. *Multiple Choice*   What is the coefficient of x^8 in the expansion of $(x + 4)^{12}$?

   Ⓐ 1056   Ⓑ 14,080

   Ⓒ 126,720   Ⓓ 811,008

   Ⓔ 3,784,704

Standardized Test Practice

For use with pages 716–722

TEST TAKING STRATEGY **Long-term preparation will definitely affect not only your standardized test scores, but your overall future academic performance as well.**

1. *Multiple Choice* What is the probability of rolling an even number if you roll a six-sided die with sides numbered from 1 through 6?

   Ⓐ $\frac{1}{6}$ Ⓑ $\frac{1}{2}$
   Ⓒ $\frac{1}{4}$ Ⓓ $\frac{1}{3}$
   Ⓔ 1

2. *Multiple Choice* What is the probability of drawing all red cards from a standard deck of 52 cards if you draw 5 cards from the deck?

   Ⓐ 0.0253   Ⓑ 0.253
   Ⓒ 0.50   Ⓓ 0.523
   Ⓔ 0.875

3. *Multiple Choice* A dart thrown at the square target shown is equally likely to hit anywhere inside the target. What is the probability that the dart hits the shaded region?

   Ⓐ $\frac{2}{3}$ Ⓑ $\frac{4}{9}$
   Ⓒ $\frac{2}{9}$ Ⓓ $\frac{8}{9}$
   Ⓔ $\frac{4}{3}$

4. *Multiple Choice* You have an equally likely chance of choosing any number from 1 to 15. What is the probability that you choose a number greater than 10?

   Ⓐ $\frac{1}{15}$ Ⓑ $\frac{1}{10}$ Ⓒ $\frac{1}{5}$
   Ⓓ $\frac{4}{5}$ Ⓔ $\frac{1}{3}$

5. *Multiple Choice* A dart thrown at the square target shown is equally likely to hit anywhere inside the target. What is the probability that the dart hits the circular shaded region?

   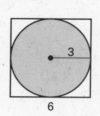

   Ⓐ $\frac{\pi}{36}$ Ⓑ $\frac{\pi}{9}$
   Ⓒ $\frac{\pi}{6}$ Ⓓ $\frac{\pi}{4}$
   Ⓔ $\frac{\pi}{2}$

6. *Multiple Choice* You have an equally likely chance of choosing any number from 1 to 10. What is the probability that you choose a number less than 4?

   Ⓐ $\frac{2}{5}$ Ⓑ $\frac{1}{2}$ Ⓒ $\frac{3}{10}$
   Ⓓ $\frac{4}{5}$ Ⓔ $\frac{2}{3}$

Quantitative Comparison **In Exercises 7 and 8, choose the statement below that is true about the given quantities if a jar contains 3 red marbles, 6 blue marbles, 5 green marbles, and 1 black marble.**

   Ⓐ The number in column A is greater.
   Ⓑ The number in column B is greater.
   Ⓒ The two numbers are equal.
   Ⓓ The relationship cannot be determined from the given information.

	Column A	Column B
7.	The probability of selecting a green marble	The probability of selecting a blue marble
8.	The probability of selecting a red or a green marble	The probability of selecting a blue or a red marble

Chapter 12

Standardized Test Practice

For use with pages 724–729

TEST TAKING STRATEGY   **The best way to prepare for a standardized test is to keep up with your day-to-day studies.**

1. *Multiple Choice*   A card is randomly selected from a standard deck of 52 cards. What is the probability that it is a 10 or a diamond?

    Ⓐ 0.504   Ⓑ 0.430

    Ⓒ 0.405   Ⓓ 0.285

    Ⓔ 0.308

2. *Multiple Choice*   A card is randomly selected from a standard deck of 52 cards. What is the probability that it is an 8 or a king?

    Ⓐ 0.25   Ⓑ 0.208

    Ⓒ 0.154   Ⓓ 0.106

    Ⓔ 0.082

3. *Multiple Choice*   When two fair coins are tossed, there are four possible outcomes. What is the probability that two heads are tossed?

    Ⓐ $\frac{1}{8}$ Ⓑ $\frac{1}{4}$ Ⓒ $\frac{1}{2}$

    Ⓓ $\frac{2}{3}$ Ⓔ $\frac{3}{8}$

4. *Multiple Choice*   When two fair coins are tossed, there are four possible outcomes. What is the probability that at least one tail is tossed?

    Ⓐ $\frac{3}{8}$ Ⓑ $\frac{1}{8}$ Ⓒ $\frac{1}{2}$

    Ⓓ $\frac{1}{4}$ Ⓔ $\frac{3}{4}$

5. *Multiple Choice*   If $P(A) = 0.4$, $P(B) = 0.2$, and $P(A \text{ and } B) = 0.18$, what is $P(A \text{ or } B)$?

    Ⓐ 0.38   Ⓑ 0.42

    Ⓒ 0.56   Ⓓ 0.58

    Ⓔ 0.61

6. *Multiple Choice*   If $P(A) = 0.28$, $P(B) = 0.41$, and $P(A \text{ and } B) = 0.16$, what is $P(A \text{ or } B)$?

    Ⓐ 0.69   Ⓑ 0.53

    Ⓒ 0.57   Ⓓ 0.44

    Ⓔ 0.03

7. *Multi-Step Problem*   A box of electrical parts contains 7 good items and 3 defective items.

    a. If 3 parts are selected at random, find the probability that all 3 parts are good.

    b. If 3 parts are selected at random, find the probability that all 3 parts are defective.

    c. If 3 parts are selected at random, find the probability that the first 2 parts are good and the third part is defective.

    d. If 2 parts are selected at random, find the probability that at least 1 part is defective.

    e. *Critical Thinking*   Explain how many parts must be selected from the box to be certain that you have at least one good part.

8. *Multiple Choice*   If $P(A) = 0.27$, $P(B) = 0.47$, and $P(A \text{ and } B) = 0.16$, what is $P(A \text{ or } B)$?

    Ⓐ 0.38   Ⓑ 0.42

    Ⓒ 0.56   Ⓓ 0.58

    Ⓔ 0.61

9. *Multiple Choice*   If $P(A) = 0.7$, $P(B) = 0.4$, and $P(A \text{ or } B) = 0.8$, what is $P(A \text{ and } B)$?

    Ⓐ 0.3   Ⓑ 0.4

    Ⓒ 0.5   Ⓓ 0.8

    Ⓔ 0.6

Standardized Test Practice

For use with pages 730–737

TEST TAKING STRATEGY **You can always return to a more difficult problem later with a fresh perspective.**

1. *Multiple Choice* Events A and B are independent, $P(A) = 0.7$, and $P(B) = 0.4$. What is $P(A \text{ and } B)$?

   Ⓐ 0.3 Ⓑ 0.28

   Ⓒ 0.72 Ⓓ 1.1

   Ⓔ 0.55

2. *Multiple Choice* Events A and B are independent, $P(A) = 0.2$, and $P(B) = 0.5$. What is $P(A \text{ and } B)$?

   Ⓐ 0.7 Ⓑ 0.3

   Ⓒ 0.1 Ⓓ 0.35

   Ⓔ 0.4

3. *Multiple Choice* Events A and B are dependent, $P(A) = 40\%$, and $P(B|A) = 30\%$. What is $P(A \text{ and } B)$?

   Ⓐ 73% Ⓑ 10%

   Ⓒ 12% Ⓓ 53%

   Ⓔ 24%

4. *Multiple Choice* Events A and B are dependent, $P(A) = 15\%$, and $P(B|A) = 60\%$. What is $P(A \text{ and } B)$?

   Ⓐ 75% Ⓑ 45% Ⓒ 38%

   Ⓓ 9% Ⓔ 90%

5. *Multiple Choice* Events A and B are independent, $P(A) = 26\%$, and $P(B) = 42\%$. What is $P(A \text{ and } B)$?

   Ⓐ 68% Ⓑ 34% Ⓒ 26%

   Ⓓ 16% Ⓔ 11%

6. *Multiple Choice* To win a state lottery, a player must correctly match six different numbers from 1 to 45. If a computer randomly assigns six numbers per ticket, how many tickets would a person have to buy to have a 1% chance of winning?

   Ⓐ at least 81,860 Ⓑ at least 8186

   Ⓒ at least 818,606 Ⓓ at least 818

   Ⓔ at least 81

Quantitative Comparison **In Exercises 7–9, choose the statement below that is true about the given quantities.**

   Ⓐ The number in column A is greater.

   Ⓑ The number in column B is greater.

   Ⓒ The two numbers are equal.

   Ⓓ The relationship cannot be determined from the given information.

	Column A	Column B
7.	The probability of drawing at least one club from a standard deck of 52 cards when drawing three times without replacement	The probability of drawing at least one club from a standard deck of 52 cards when drawing three times with replacement
8.	The probability of tossing a head using a fair coin if a head has already been tossed	The probability of tossing a tail using a fair coin if a head has already been tossed
9.	The probability of tossing at least one head when tossing a fair coin two times	The probability of tossing at most one tail when tossing a fair coin two times

Standardized Test Practice

For use with pages 739–744

TEST TAKING STRATEGY   **If you get stuck on a question, look at the answer choices for clues.**

1. Multiple Choice   What is the probability of tossing a coin 10 times and getting exactly 4 heads?

Ⓐ 0.18   Ⓑ 0.21

Ⓒ 0.27   Ⓓ 0.32

Ⓔ 0.36

2. Multiple Choice   What is the probability of tossing a coin 20 times and getting exactly 16 tails?

Ⓐ 0.176   Ⓑ 0.160

Ⓒ 0.015   Ⓓ 0.005

Ⓔ 0.001

3. Multiple Choice   What is the probability that in a family of six children exactly four are boys? Assume a boy and a girl are equally likely.

Ⓐ $\frac{2}{3}$ Ⓑ $\frac{1}{3}$

Ⓒ $\frac{5}{32}$ Ⓓ $\frac{11}{64}$

Ⓔ $\frac{15}{64}$

4. Multiple Choice   What is the probability that in a family of seven children exactly two are girls? Assume a boy and a girl are equally likely.

Ⓐ $\frac{21}{128}$ Ⓑ $\frac{7}{64}$

Ⓒ $\frac{7}{128}$ Ⓓ $\frac{5}{7}$

Ⓔ $\frac{2}{7}$

5. Multiple Choice   What is the probability of 5 or more successes for a binomial experiment consisting of 7 trials with probability 0.25 of success on each trial?

Ⓐ 0.0115   Ⓑ 0.0129

Ⓒ 0.0128   Ⓓ 0.0577

Ⓔ 0.0013

Quantitative Comparison   In Exercises 6–8, choose the statement below that is true about the given quantities in calculating the probability of *k* successes for a binomial experiment consisting of *n* trials with probability *p* of success on each trial.

Ⓐ   The number in column A is greater.

Ⓑ   The number in column B is greater.

Ⓒ   The two numbers are equal.

Ⓓ   The relationship cannot be determined from the given information.

	Column A	Column B
6.	$k \geq 2, n = 4,$ $p = 0.6$	$k \leq 2, n = 6,$ $p = 0.8$
7.	$k \geq 3, n = 8,$ $p = 0.37$	$k \geq 5, n = 6,$ $p = 0.21$
8.	$k \leq 3, n = 5,$ $p = 0.4$	$k \leq 4, n = 5,$ $p = 0.42$

9. Multiple Choice   A baseball player's batting average is 0.280. What is the probability that the player will get 3 or fewer hits in a game in which the player has 5 official at-bats?

Ⓐ 0.376   Ⓑ 0.293

Ⓒ 0.783   Ⓓ 0.114

Ⓔ 0.976

10. Multiple Choice   What is the probability of 2 or fewer successes for a binomial experiment consisting of 6 trials with probability 0.52 of success on each trial?

Ⓐ 0.942   Ⓑ 0.781

Ⓒ 0.559   Ⓓ 0.483

Ⓔ 0.307

Algebra 2
Standardized Test Practice Workbook

TEST TAKING STRATEGY **Do not panic if you run out of time before answering all of the questions. You can still receive a high score on a standardized test without answering every question.**

1. *Multiple Choice* What is the probability that a randomly selected *x*-value lies between 6 and 10 if the normal distribution has a mean of 7 and a standard deviation of 1?

   Ⓐ 0.68   Ⓑ 0.815

   Ⓒ 0.8385   Ⓓ 0.4985

   Ⓔ 0.3635

2. *Multiple Choice* What is the probability that a randomly selected *x*-value lies between 7 and 9 if the normal distribution has a mean of 6 and a standard deviation of 1?

   Ⓐ 0.815   Ⓑ 0.4985

   Ⓒ 0.8385   Ⓓ 0.5

   Ⓔ 0.1585

3. *Multiple Choice* What is the probability that a randomly selected *x*-value is at least 10 if the normal distribution has a mean of 8 and a standard deviation of 1?

   Ⓐ 0.95   Ⓑ 0.815

   Ⓒ 0.025   Ⓓ 0.5

   Ⓔ 0.1585

4. *Multiple Choice* What is the mean of a normal distribution that approximates a binomial distribution consisting of 15 trials with probability 0.6 of success on each trial?

   Ⓐ 6   Ⓑ 7   Ⓒ 8

   Ⓓ 9   Ⓔ 10

5. *Multiple Choice* What is the mean of a normal distribution that approximates a binomial distribution consisting of 25 trials with probability 0.4 of success on each trial?

   Ⓐ 5   Ⓑ 10   Ⓒ 15

   Ⓓ 20   Ⓔ 25

6. *Multiple Choice* What is the standard deviation of a normal distribution that approximates a binomial distribution consisting of 30 trials with probability 0.2 of success on each trial?

   Ⓐ 1.76   Ⓑ 1.92

   Ⓒ 2.08   Ⓓ 2.19

   Ⓔ 2.27

7. *Multi-Step Problem* In 1999 Sarah took both the SAT (Scholastic Aptitude Test) and the ACT (American College Test). On the mathematics section of the SAT, she earned a score of 630. On the mathematics section of the ACT, she earned a score of 30. For the SAT the mean was 480 and the standard deviation was 75. For the ACT the mean was 26 and the standard deviation was 4.

   a. What percent of students did Sarah outscore on the math section of the SAT?

   b. What percent of students did Sarah outscore on the math section of the ACT?

   c. On which exam did Sarah score better?

   d. *Writing* Explain how you could translate SAT scores such as 255, 330, and 405 into equivalent ACT scores if you know the mean and standard deviation of each exam.

8. *Multiple Choice* What is the standard deviation of a normal distribution that approximates a binomial distribution consisting of 50 trials with probability 0.3 of success on each trial?

   Ⓐ 3.65   Ⓑ 3.24

   Ⓒ 2.86   Ⓓ 2.52

   Ⓔ 2.28

Chapter 12

TEST TAKING STRATEGY   **Try to find shortcuts that will help you move through the questions quicker.**

1. *Multiple Choice*   Given the diagram, which equation is correct?

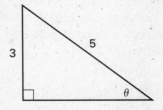

Ⓐ $\sin \theta = \dfrac{5}{3}$ Ⓑ $\cos \theta = \dfrac{3}{4}$

Ⓒ $\sec \theta = \dfrac{5}{4}$ Ⓓ $\tan \theta = \dfrac{4}{3}$

Ⓔ $\cot \theta = \dfrac{3}{5}$

2. *Multiple Choice*   Given the diagram, which equation is correct?

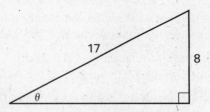

Ⓐ $\sin \theta = \dfrac{8}{17}$ Ⓑ $\cos \theta = \dfrac{8}{15}$

Ⓒ $\sec \theta = \dfrac{15}{17}$ Ⓓ $\tan \theta = \dfrac{17}{15}$

Ⓔ $\csc \theta = \dfrac{15}{8}$

3. *Multiple Choice*   Given the diagram, what is the value of x?

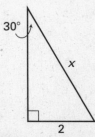

Ⓐ 8

Ⓑ 6.5

Ⓒ 4.8

Ⓓ 6.9

Ⓔ 4

4. *Multiple Choice*   Given the diagram, what is the value of x?

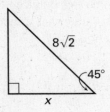

Ⓐ 5.66

Ⓑ 4.87

Ⓒ 4

Ⓓ 8

Ⓔ $4\sqrt{2}$

5. *Multiple Choice*   Given the diagram where $A = 36°$ and $a = 8$ cm, what is the approximate value of c?

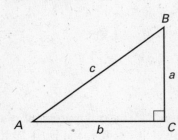

Ⓐ 0.073 cm

Ⓑ 13.6 cm

Ⓒ 14.9 cm

Ⓓ 9.7 cm

Ⓔ 10.8 cm

6. *Multi-Step Problem*   You are a surveyor in a helicopter and are trying to determine the width of an island, as illustrated.

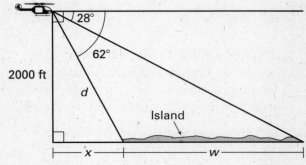

a. What is the shortest distance d the helicopter would have to travel to land on the island?

b. What is the horizontal distance x that the helicopter has to travel before it is directly over the nearer end of the island?

c. *Writing*   Find the width w of the island. Explain the process you used to find your answer.

Chapter 13

Standardized Test Practice

For use with pages 776–783

TEST TAKING STRATEGY   Read the test questions carefully.

1. *Multiple Choice*   Which of the following is a coterminal angle with $-150°$?

   Ⓐ 150°   Ⓑ 210°   Ⓒ $-30°$

   Ⓓ $-210°$ Ⓔ 30°

2. *Multiple Choice*   Which of the following is a coterminal angle with 326°?

   Ⓐ $-34°$ Ⓑ 168°   Ⓒ 34°

   Ⓓ $-326°$ Ⓔ 122°

3. *Multiple Choice*   Which of the following is equivalent to $\frac{7\pi}{4}$?

   Ⓐ 285°   Ⓑ 305°   Ⓒ 315°

   Ⓓ 330°   Ⓔ 375°

4. *Multiple Choice*   Which of the following is equivalent to 240°?

   Ⓐ $\frac{5\pi}{6}$ Ⓑ $\frac{8\pi}{3}$ Ⓒ $\frac{5\pi}{4}$

   Ⓓ $\frac{7\pi}{6}$ Ⓔ $\frac{4\pi}{3}$

5. *Multiple Choice*   What is the arc length of a sector with a radius of 5 cm and a central angle of 20°?

   Ⓐ 100 cm   Ⓑ 4 cm   Ⓒ 1.75 cm

   Ⓓ 2.8 cm   Ⓔ 4.35 cm

6. *Multiple Choice*   What is the arc length of a sector with a radius of 7.3 in. and a central angle of 66°?

   Ⓐ 6.7 in.   Ⓑ 7.3 in.   Ⓒ 8.4 in.

   Ⓓ 8.9 in.   Ⓔ 10.5 in.

7. *Multiple Choice*   What is the area of a sector with a radius of 10 cm and a central angle of 50°?

   Ⓐ 40.08 cm²   Ⓑ 43.63 cm²

   Ⓒ 48.72 cm²   Ⓓ 51.43 cm²

   Ⓔ 58.18 cm²

Quantitative Comparison   **In Exercises 8–11, choose the statement below that is true about the given quantities.**

   Ⓐ The number in column A is greater.

   Ⓑ The number in column B is greater.

   Ⓒ The two numbers are equal.

   Ⓓ The relationship cannot be determined from the given information.

	Column A	Column B
8.	The area of a sector with $r = 3$ in. and $\theta = 45°$	The area of a sector with $r = 4$ in. and $\theta = 60°$
9.	The area of a sector with $r = 11.3$ cm and $\theta = 100°$	The area of a sector with $r = 12.6$ cm and $\theta = 82°$
10.	The arc length of a sector with $r = 8$ ft and $\theta = 120°$	The arc length of a sector with $r = 4$ ft and $\theta = 240°$
11.	The arc length of a sector with $r = 2$ m and $\theta = \frac{8\pi}{3}$	The arc length of a sector with $r = 6$ m and $\theta = \frac{2\pi}{3}$

Chapter 13

Standardized Test Practice
For use with pages 784–790

TEST TAKING STRATEGY   **Some college entrance exams allow the optional use of calculators. If you do use a calculator, make sure it is one you are familiar with and have used before.**

1. *Multiple Choice*   If $(6, 2)$ is a point on the terminal side of an angle θ in standard position, what is the value of $\sin \theta$?

   (A) $\sqrt{10}$ (B) 3 (C) $\dfrac{2}{\sqrt{10}}$

   (D) $\dfrac{1}{\sqrt{10}}$ (E) $\dfrac{1}{3}$

2. *Multiple Choice*   If $(-10, 8)$ is a point on the terminal side of an angle θ in standard position, what is the value of $\tan \theta$?

   (A) $4\sqrt{21}$ (B) $-\dfrac{4}{5}$ (C) $-5\sqrt{21}$

   (D) $-\dfrac{5}{4}$ (E) $5\sqrt{21}$

3. *Multiple Choice*   Which of the following is the reference angle for $\theta = 158°$?

   (A) $58°$ (B) $22°$ (C) $202°$

   (D) $-202°$ (E) $-22°$

4. *Multiple Choice*   Which of the following is the reference angle for

   $\theta = -\dfrac{3\pi}{5}$?

   (A) $\dfrac{2\pi}{5}$ (B) $\dfrac{\pi}{5}$ (C) $\dfrac{3\pi}{10}$

   (D) $\dfrac{7\pi}{5}$ (E) $\dfrac{8\pi}{5}$

5. *Multiple Choice*   What is the exact value of $\tan 390°$?

   (A) $\sqrt{3}$ (B) $\dfrac{1}{3}$ (C) $3\sqrt{3}$

   (D) $-\sqrt{3}$ (E) $\dfrac{\sqrt{3}}{3}$

6. *Multiple Choice*   What is the exact value of $\cos\left(-\dfrac{13\pi}{4}\right)$?

   (A) $\dfrac{\sqrt{2}}{2}$ (B) $\sqrt{2}$ (C) $-\dfrac{\sqrt{2}}{2}$

   (D) $-\sqrt{2}$ (E) $\dfrac{1}{2}$

7. *Multiple Choice*   What is the approximate horizontal distance traveled by a soccer ball that is kicked at an angle of 30° with an initial speed of 60 feet per second?

   (A) 84 ft   (B) 88 ft   (C) 93 ft

   (D) 97 ft   (E) 105 ft

Quantitative Comparison   **In Exercises 8–11, choose the statement below that is true about the given quantities.**

   (A) The number in column A is greater.

   (B) The number in column B is greater.

   (C) The two numbers are equal.

   (D) The relationship cannot be determined from the given information.

	Column A	Column B
8.	The value of $\sin 630°$	The value of $\tan 125°$
9.	The value of $\cos\left(-\dfrac{11\pi}{3}\right)$	The value of $\sec \dfrac{5\pi}{3}$
10.	The value of $\cot(-278°)$	The value of $\csc(134°)$
11.	The value of $\cos \dfrac{3\pi}{4}$	The value of $\sin \dfrac{7\pi}{4}$

Chapter 13

NAME _____ DATE _____

Standardized Test Practice

For use with pages 791–798

1. Multiple Choice Which angle does the value of $\tan^{-1}\left(-\dfrac{\sqrt{3}}{3}\right)$ equal?

Ⓐ 210°   Ⓑ 150°   Ⓒ 330°

Ⓓ 300°   Ⓔ 30°

2. Multiple Choice Which angle does the value of $\sin^{-1}\left(\dfrac{1}{\sqrt{2}}\right)$ equal?

Ⓐ 45°   Ⓑ 225°   Ⓒ 175°

Ⓓ 345°   Ⓔ 305°

3. Multiple Choice In the triangle shown, what is the approximate measure of the angle θ?

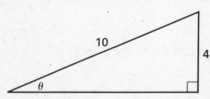

Ⓐ 23.6°   Ⓑ 21.8°   Ⓒ 34.4°

Ⓓ 66.4°   Ⓔ 82.5°

4. Multiple Choice In the triangle shown, what is the approximate measure of the angle θ?

Ⓐ 13.8°   Ⓑ 15.3°   Ⓒ 22.6°

Ⓓ 74.2°   Ⓔ 74.7°

5. Multiple Choice What is the solution of the equation $\cos \theta = -\dfrac{1}{5}$ where $180° < \theta < 270°$?

Ⓐ 192.17°   Ⓑ 198.23°   Ⓒ 213.67°

Ⓓ 243.61°   Ⓔ 258.46°

6. Multiple Choice What is the solution of $\tan \theta = -3.732$ where $\dfrac{3\pi}{2} < \theta < 2\pi$?

Ⓐ $\dfrac{5\pi}{3}$ Ⓑ $\dfrac{11\pi}{6}$ Ⓒ $\dfrac{19\pi}{12}$

Ⓓ $\dfrac{23\pi}{12}$ Ⓔ $\dfrac{5\pi}{12}$

7. Multi-Step Problem If you stand in shallow water and look at an object below the surface of the water, the object will look farther away from you than it really is. This is because when light rays pass between air and water, the water *refracts*, or bends, the light rays. The *index of refraction* for seawater is 1.341. This is the ratio of the sine of θ_1 to the sine of θ_2 for angles θ_1 and θ_2 below.

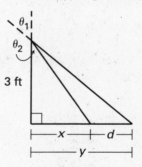

a. You are standing in seawater that is 3 feet deep and are looking at a shell at an angle $\theta_1 = 50°$ (measured from a line perpendicular to the surface of the water). Find θ_2.

b. Find the distances x and y.

c. Find the distance d between where the shell is and where it appears to be.

d. **Writing** What happens to d as you move closer to the shell?

Standardized Test Practice

For use with pages 799–806

TEST TAKING STRATEGY   If you find yourself spending too much time on one question and getting frustrated, move on to the next question.

1. *Multiple Choice*   What is the approximate value of *b* in the triangle shown?

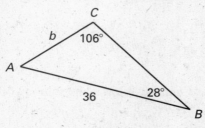

  Ⓐ 28.3   Ⓑ 22.7   Ⓒ 18.5

  Ⓓ 17.6   Ⓔ 16.4

2. *Multiple Choice*   What is the approximate value of *c* in the triangle shown?

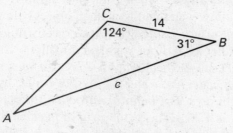

  Ⓐ 29.3   Ⓑ 27.5   Ⓒ 25.1

  Ⓓ 24.8   Ⓔ 23.4

3. *Multiple Choice*   What is the approximate value of *a* in the triangle shown?

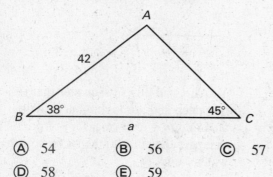

  Ⓐ 54   Ⓑ 56   Ⓒ 57

  Ⓓ 58   Ⓔ 59

4. *Multiple Choice*   What is the approximate measure of angle *A* in the triangle shown?

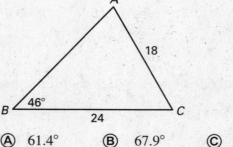

  Ⓐ 61.4°   Ⓑ 67.9°   Ⓒ 73.6°

  Ⓓ 81.5°   Ⓔ 106.7°

5. *Multiple Choice*   What is the approximate area of a triangle with $A = 22°$, $b = 14$, and $c = 27$?

  Ⓐ 70.8 units^2 Ⓑ 72.3 units^2

  Ⓒ 74.6 units^2 Ⓓ 77.9 units^2

  Ⓔ 82.1 units^2

6. *Multi-Step Problem*   You are at an unknown distance *d* from a mountain, as shown at the right. The angle of elevation to the top of the mountain is 72°. You step back 85 feet and measure the angle of elevation to be 63°.

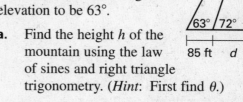

a.   Find the height *h* of the mountain using the law of sines and right triangle trigonometry. (*Hint*: First find θ.)

b.   Find the height *h* of the mountain using a system of equations. Set up one tangent equation involving the ratio of *d* and *h*, and another tangent equation involving the ratio of 85 + *d* and *h* and then solve the system.

c.   *Writing*   Which method was easier for you to use? Explain.

TEST TAKING STRATEGY   **If you get stuck on a question, select an answer choice and check to see if it is a reasonable answer to the question.**

1. *Multiple Choice*   In the triangle shown, what is the approximate length of *b*?

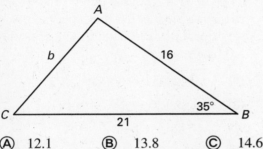

   Ⓐ 12.1   Ⓑ 13.8   Ⓒ 14.6

   Ⓓ 16.9   Ⓔ 20.3

2. *Multiple Choice*   In the triangle shown, what is the approximate length of *c*?

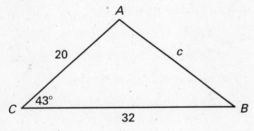

   Ⓐ 18.6   Ⓑ 21.4   Ⓒ 22.1

   Ⓓ 23.8   Ⓔ 25.7

3. *Multiple Choice*   What is the approximate measure of angle *A* in a triangle with $a = 10$, $b = 25$, and $c = 18$?

   Ⓐ 18.6°   Ⓑ 19.4°   Ⓒ 20.3°

   Ⓓ 22.6°   Ⓔ 37.5°

4. *Multiple Choice*   What is the approximate measure of angle *C* in a triangle with $a = 21$, $b = 14$, and $c = 28$?

   Ⓐ 83.7°   Ⓑ 92.1°   Ⓒ 98.6°

   Ⓓ 103.2°   Ⓔ 104.5°

5. *Multiple Choice*   What is the approximate area of a triangle with $a = 23$, $b = 38$, and $c = 47$?

   Ⓐ 381 units²   Ⓑ 417 units²

   Ⓒ 433 units²   Ⓓ 452 units²

   Ⓔ 489 units²

6. *Multiple Choice*   What is the approximate area of a triangle with $a = 10$ ft, $b = 15$ ft, and $c = 21$ ft?

   Ⓐ 69.2 ft²   Ⓑ 70.8 ft²

   Ⓒ 71.4 ft²   Ⓓ 78.3 ft²

   Ⓔ 82.5 ft²

Quantitative Comparison   **In Exercises 7–10, choose the statement below that is true about the given quantities.**

   Ⓐ   The number in column A is greater.

   Ⓑ   The number in column B is greater.

   Ⓒ   The two numbers are equal.

   Ⓓ   The relationship cannot be determined from the given information.

	Column A	Column B
7.	The area of a triangle with $a = 6$, $b = 10$, and $c = 8$	The area of a triangle with $a = 3$, $b = 4$, and $c = 5$
8.	The area of a triangle with $a = 12$, $b = 16$, and $c = 18$	The area of a triangle with $a = 15$, $b = 10$, and $c = 23$
9.	The measure of angle A in a triangle with $a = 42$, $b = 31$, and $c = 28$	The measure of angle B in a triangle with $a = 11$, $b = 23$, and $c = 19$
10.	The length of side b in a triangle with $a = 8$, $c = 13$, and $B = 40°$	The length of side c in a triangle with $a = 12$, $b = 18$, and $C = 68°$

Chapter 13

TEST TAKING STRATEGY **If the answers to a question are formulas, substitute the given numbers into the formulas to test the possible answers.**

1. *Multiple Choice* Which set of parametric equations is graphed?

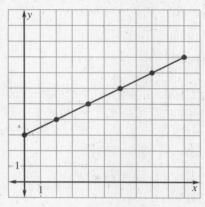

  Ⓐ $x = 2t,\ y = t + 3$ for $0 \le t \le 5$

  Ⓑ $x = \dfrac{1}{2}t,\ y = t$ for $0 \le t \le 5$

  Ⓒ $x = t + 2,\ y = t$ for $0 \le t \le 5$

  Ⓓ $x = 4t,\ y = t - 3$ for $0 \le t \le 5$

  Ⓔ $x = 2t + 1,\ y = 3t$ for $0 \le t \le 5$

2. *Multiple Choice* Which equation is an *xy*-equation for the parametric equations $x = t + 3$ and $y = 2t - 1$ where $0 \le t \le 10$?

  Ⓐ $y = x - 4;\ 0 \le x \le 10$

  Ⓑ $y = 3x + 2;\ 10 \le x \le 20$

  Ⓒ $y = 2x - 3;\ 3 \le x \le 19$

  Ⓓ $y = 2x - 7;\ 3 \le x \le 13$

  Ⓔ $y = -x - 4;\ 0 \le x \le -10$

3. *Multiple Choice* An airplane takes off at an angle of 11.8° with the ground and travels at a constant speed of 286 miles per hour. Which set of parametric equations represents the airplane's ascent?

  Ⓐ $x = 2840t,\ y = 500t$

  Ⓑ $x = 280t,\ y = 58t$

  Ⓒ $x = 320t,\ y = 64t$

  Ⓓ $x = 1260t,\ y = 840t$

  Ⓔ $x = 560t,\ y = 76t$

Quantitative Comparison **In Exercises 4–8, choose the statement below that is true about the given quantities.**

  Ⓐ   The number in column A is greater.

  Ⓑ   The number in column B is greater.

  Ⓒ   The two numbers are equal.

  Ⓓ   The relationship cannot be determined from the given information.

	Column A	Column B
4.	The value of x if $x = 6.5 \cos 30°$	The value of x if $x = 6.5 \sin 30°$
5.	The value of x if $x = (4.8 \cos 45°)t$ and $t = 3$	The value of x if $x = (4.8 \sin 45°)t$ and $t = 3$
6.	The value of x if $x = (1.6 \cos 18°)t$ and $t = 4$	The value of x if $x = (1.6 \sin 39°)t$ and $t = 6$
7.	The value of x if $x = (5.2 \cos 22°)t$ and $t = 2$	The value of x if $x = (5.2 \sin 68°)t$ and $t = 2$
8.	The value of x if $x = (2.3 \cos 65°)t$ and $t = 3$	The value of x if $x = (2.3 \sin 38°)t$ and $t = 5$

Chapter 13

Standardized Test Practice

For use with pages 831–837

TEST TAKING STRATEGY   **Draw an arrow on your test booklet next to questions that you do not answer. This will enable you to find the questions quickly when you go back.**

1. *Multiple Choice*   Which function is graphed?

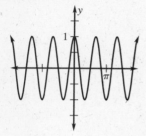

(A) $y = \sin 3x$ (B) $y = 3 \cos 3x$
(C) $y = \cos 3x$ (D) $y = 3 \sin 3x$
(E) $y = \cos \frac{1}{3}x$

2. *Multiple Choice*   Which function is graphed?

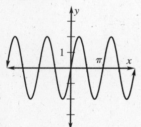

(A) $y = \sin 2x$ (B) $y = 2 \cos 2x$
(C) $y = \cos 2x$ (D) $y = \sin \frac{1}{2}x$
(E) $y = 2 \sin 2x$

3. *Multiple Choice*   Which of the following is an x-intercept of the graph of $y = \frac{1}{2} \sin \frac{\pi}{3}x$?

(A) 6   (B) 5   (C) -4
(D) 1   (E) 3π

4. *Multiple Choice*   Which of the following is an x-intercept of the graph of $y = 2 \cos \frac{\pi}{4}x$?

(A) 2   (B) 3   (C) 4
(D) 5π (E) -4

5. *Multiple Choice*   What is the amplitude of the graph of $y = -3 \cos 2x$?

(A) -3 (B) 3   (C) 2
(D) -2 (E) -6

6. *Multiple Choice*   What is the period of the graph of $y = \frac{1}{4} \sin 3x$?

(A) 3π (B) $\frac{\pi}{2}$ (C) $\frac{3\pi}{4}$
(D) $\frac{2\pi}{3}$ (E) $\frac{3}{4}$

Quantitative Comparison   **In Exercises 7 and 8, choose the statement below that is true about the given quanitites.**

(A)   The number in column A is greater.

(B)   The number in column B is greater.

(C)   The two numbers are equal.

(D)   The relationship cannot be determined from the given information.

	Column A	Column B
7.	Amplitude of the graph of $y = -5 \cos 3x$	Amplitude of the graph of $y = 5 \sin 5x$
8.	Period of the graph of $y = \frac{1}{2} \tan 2\pi x$	Period of the graph of $y = 3 \sin 8\pi x$

Chapter 14

TEST TAKING STRATEGY   **The mathematical portion of a standardized test is based on concepts and skills taught in high school mathematics courses.**

1. *Multiple Choice*   Which function is graphed?

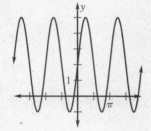

Ⓐ $y = 2 + 3 \sin 2x$ Ⓑ $y = 3 \sin 2x$

Ⓒ $y = 2 + 3 \cos 2x$ Ⓓ $y = 2 - 3 \sin 2x$

Ⓔ $y = -2 + 3 \cos 2x$

2. *Multiple Choice*   Which function is graphed?

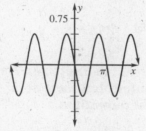

Ⓐ $y = \frac{1}{2} \sin 2\left(x + \frac{\pi}{4}\right)$

Ⓑ $y = \frac{1}{2} \cos 2\left(x - \frac{\pi}{4}\right)$

Ⓒ $y = -\frac{1}{2} \cos 2\left(x + \frac{\pi}{4}\right)$

Ⓓ $y = \frac{1}{2} \cos 2\left(x + \frac{\pi}{4}\right)$

Ⓔ $y = \frac{1}{2} \sin 2\left(x - \frac{\pi}{4}\right)$

3. *Multiple Choice*   Which of the following functions represents the reflection of the graph of $y = 5 \sin 3x$?

Ⓐ $y = -5 \sin 3x$ Ⓑ $y = 5 \sin \frac{1}{3}x$

Ⓒ $y = \frac{1}{5} \sin 3x$ Ⓓ $y = 3 \sin 5x$

Ⓔ $y = 5 \sin (-3x)$

4. *Multiple Choice*   Which of the following functions represents a vertical shift up of the graph of $y = \frac{1}{3} \cos \frac{2}{3}x$?

Ⓐ $y = -\frac{1}{3} \cos \frac{2}{3}x$

Ⓑ $y = \frac{1}{3} \cos \frac{3}{2}x$

Ⓒ $y = 1 + \frac{1}{3} \cos \frac{2}{3}x$

Ⓓ $y = -2 + \frac{1}{3} \cos \frac{2}{3}x$

Ⓔ $y = \frac{1}{3} \cos \frac{2}{3}\left(x - \frac{\pi}{6}\right)$

5. *Multiple-Step Problem*   You are at the top of a 160 foot building that straddles a road. You are looking down at a truck traveling straight toward the building.

   a.   Write an equation of the truck's distance from the base of the building as a function of the angle of depression from you to the truck.

   b.   Suppose the truck is between you and a large road sign that you know is 3500 feet from the building. Write an equation for the distance between the road sign and the truck as a function of the angle of depression from you to the truck.

   c.   Graph the functions you wrote in parts (a) and (b) in the same coordinate plane.

   d.   *Writing*   Describe how the graphs you drew in part (c) are geometrically related.

NAME _____ DATE _____

Standardized Test Practice

For use with pages 848–854

TEST TAKING STRATEGY   Even though you must keep your answer sheet neat, you can make any kind of mark you want in your test booklet.

1. **Multiple Choice**   Which of the following is equal to cos 48°?

   Ⓐ cos 42°   Ⓑ sin 48°

   Ⓒ tan 48°   Ⓓ tan 42°

   Ⓔ sin 42°

2. **Multiple Choice**   Which of the following is equal to $\tan\left(-\dfrac{\pi}{4}\right)$?

   Ⓐ $\tan\left(\dfrac{\pi}{4}\right)$ Ⓑ $\sin\left(\dfrac{\pi}{4}\right)$

   Ⓒ $-\tan\left(\dfrac{\pi}{4}\right)$ Ⓓ $\cos\left(-\dfrac{\pi}{4}\right)$

   Ⓔ $-\cos\left(\dfrac{\pi}{4}\right)$

3. **Multiple Choice**   If $\cos\theta = -\dfrac{4}{5}$ and

   $\pi < \theta < \dfrac{3\pi}{2}$, which of the following is true?

   Ⓐ $\sin\theta = -\dfrac{5}{4}$ Ⓑ $\tan\theta = \dfrac{3}{4}$

   Ⓒ $\tan\theta = -\dfrac{4}{3}$ Ⓓ $\cot\theta = -\dfrac{3}{4}$

   Ⓔ $\sin\theta = \dfrac{3}{5}$

4. **Multiple Choice**   If $\tan\theta = -\dfrac{8}{15}$ and

   $\dfrac{\pi}{2} < \theta < \pi$, which of the following is true?

   Ⓐ $\sin\theta = -\dfrac{15}{17}$ Ⓑ $\sin\theta = \dfrac{8}{17}$

   Ⓒ $\csc\theta = -\dfrac{15}{8}$ Ⓓ $\sec\theta = \dfrac{17}{8}$

   Ⓔ $\cos\theta = \dfrac{15}{17}$

5. **Multiple Choice**   What is simplified form of

   $\sin\left(\dfrac{\pi}{2} - \theta\right)\tan\theta$?

   Ⓐ $\sin\theta$ Ⓑ $\cos\theta$ Ⓒ $\sec\theta$

   Ⓓ $\sin^2\theta$ Ⓔ $\tan^2\theta$

6. **Multiple Choice**   What is the simplified

   form of $\dfrac{\cos\theta}{1 - \sin^2\theta}$?

   Ⓐ $\sin\theta$ Ⓑ $\cos\theta$ Ⓒ $\sec\theta$

   Ⓓ $\cot\theta$ Ⓔ $\cos^2\theta$

7. **Multi-Step Problem**   You and Roger are riding exercise machines that involve pedaling. The following parametric equations describe the motion of your feet and Roger's feet.

YOU:	ROGER:
$x = 6\cos 2\pi t$	$x = 4\cos 3\pi t$
$y = 6\sin 2\pi t$	$y = 2\sin 3\pi t$

   In each case, x and y are measured in inches and t is measured in seconds.

   a. Use the Pythagorean identity $\sin^2\theta + \cos^2\theta = 1$ to eliminate the parameter t and simplify each expression.

   b. Use the expressions found in part (a) to describe the paths followed by your feet and Roger's feet.

   c. Find the reciprocal of the common period of the corresponding parametric functions.

   d. **Writing**   Explain who is pedaling faster (in revolutions per second) using part (c).

Standardized Test Practice

For use with pages 855–861

TEST TAKING STRATEGY   **During a test, draw graphs and figures in your test booklet to help you solve problems.**

1. *Multiple Choice*   What is a solution of the equation $4 \cos x + 2 = 0$?

   (A) $\dfrac{2\pi}{3}$ (B) $\dfrac{\pi}{6}$ (C) $\dfrac{5\pi}{3}$

   (D) $\dfrac{\pi}{4}$ (E) $\dfrac{3\pi}{4}$

2. *Multiple Choice*   What is a solution of the equation $6 \cos x - 6 = 0$?

   (A) $\dfrac{\pi}{4}$ (B) $\dfrac{2\pi}{3}$ (C) $\dfrac{3\pi}{4}$

   (D) 2π (E) $\dfrac{5\pi}{6}$

3. *Multiple Choice*   What is a solution of the equation $5 \tan x - 5 = 0$?

   (A) $-\dfrac{\pi}{4}$ (B) $\dfrac{\pi}{6}$ (C) $-\dfrac{3\pi}{4}$

   (D) $\dfrac{\pi}{12}$ (E) $-\dfrac{4\pi}{5}$

4. *Multiple Choice*   What is an approximate solution of the equation $1 - 3 \sin^2 x = 0$?

   (A) 0.583   (B) 0.615   (C) 0.672

   (D) 0.774   (E) 0.832

5. *Multiple Choice*   What is an approximate solution of the equation $2 \tan^2 x - 3 = 0$?

   (A) 0.8423   (B) 0.8571

   (C) 0.8725   (D) 0.8861

   (E) 0.8973

6. *Multiple Choice*   What is a solution of the equation $\sin x = \sqrt{3} \cos x$?

   (A) $\dfrac{\pi}{3}$ (B) $\dfrac{\pi}{6}$ (C) $\dfrac{2\pi}{3}$

   (D) $\dfrac{\pi}{4}$ (E) $\dfrac{5\pi}{4}$

Quantitative Comparison   **In Exercises 7–9, choose the statement below that is true about the given quantities.**

   (A)   The number in column A is greater.

   (B)   The number in column B is greater.

   (C)   The two numbers are equal.

   (D)   The relationship cannot be determined from the given information.

	Column A	Column B
7.	The x-intercept of the graph of $y = 2 \sin x + 1$ in the interval $0 \le x \le \dfrac{3\pi}{2}$	The x-intercept of the graph of $y = 2 \cos x + 1$ in the interval $0 \le x \le \pi$
8.	The x-intercept of the graph of $y = \dfrac{1}{2} \tan x$ in the interval $-\dfrac{\pi}{2} \le x \le \dfrac{\pi}{2}$	The x-intercept of the graph of $y = -3 \sin x$ in the interval $-\dfrac{\pi}{2} \le x \le \dfrac{\pi}{2}$
9.	The x-intercept of the graph of $y = \sin^2 x - 1$ in the interval $0 \le x \le \pi$	The x-intercept of the graph of $y = \cos^2 x$ in the interval $0 \le x \le \pi$

NAME _____ DATE _____

Standardized Test Practice

For use with pages 862–868

TEST TAKING STRATEGY   **Long-term preparation for a standardized test can be done throughout your high school career and can improve your overall abilities.**

1. *Multiple Choice*   During one cycle, a sinusoid has a minimum at $(14, 28)$ and a maximum at $(6, 46)$. What is the amplitude of the sinusoid?

   Ⓐ 4   Ⓑ 8   Ⓒ 9
   Ⓓ 13   Ⓔ 18

2. *Multiple Choice*   During one cycle, a sinusoid has a minimum at $(-4, -10)$ and a maximum at $(12, 32)$. What is the amplitude of the sinusoid?

   Ⓐ 8   Ⓑ 16   Ⓒ 22
   Ⓓ 42   Ⓔ 21

3. *Multiple Choice*   During one cycle, a sinusoid has a maximum at $(6, 18)$ and a minimum at $(2, -4)$. What is the period of the sinusoid?

   Ⓐ 8π Ⓑ 8   Ⓒ 11π
   Ⓓ 11   Ⓔ 22

4. *Multiple Choice*   During one cycle, a sinusoid has a maximum at $(-15, 21)$ and a minimum at $(21, -14)$. What is the period of the sinusoid?

   Ⓐ 18π Ⓑ 18   Ⓒ 36π
   Ⓓ 36   Ⓔ 72

5. *Multiple Choice*   Which is a function for the sinusoid with a maximum at $(0, 2)$ and a minimum at $\left(\dfrac{\pi}{2}, -2\right)$?

   Ⓐ $y = 2 \cos 2x$ Ⓑ $y = \cos 2x$
   Ⓒ $y = 2 \sin 2x$ Ⓓ $y = \sin 2x$
   Ⓔ $y = 2 \cos x$

6. *Multiple Choice*   Which is a function for the sinusoid with a maximum at $\left(\dfrac{3\pi}{8}, 5\right)$ and a minimum at $\left(\dfrac{\pi}{8}, -1\right)$?

   Ⓐ $y = \sin 4x + 2$
   Ⓑ $y = -3 \sin 4x - 2$
   Ⓒ $y = -3 \sin 4x + 2$
   Ⓓ $y = -3 \cos 4x + 2$
   Ⓔ $y = 3 \cos 4x + 2$

Quantitative Comparison   **In Exercises 7–9, choose the statement below that is true about the given quantities.**

   Ⓐ   The number in column A is greater.
   Ⓑ   The number in column B is greater.
   Ⓒ   The two numbers are equal.
   Ⓓ   The relationship cannot be determined from the given information.

	Column A	Column B
7.	Amplitude of the sinusoid with a maximum at $(-5, 18)$ and a minimum at $(7, -18)$	Amplitude of the sinusoid with a maximum at $(12, 56)$ and a minimum at $(1, 38)$
8.	Amplitude of the sinusoid with a maximum at $(\pi, 4)$ and a minimum at $(-\pi, 2)$	Amplititude of the sinusoid with a maximum at $(\pi, 9)$ and a minimum at $(0, 7)$
9.	Period of the sinusoid with a maximum at $(-5, 18)$ and a minimum at $(7, -18)$	Period of the sinusoid with a maximum at $(12, 56)$ and a minimum at $(1, 38)$

Standardized Test Practice

For use with pages 869–874

TEST TAKING STRATEGY **Some college entrance exams allow the optional use of calculators. If you do use a calculator, make sure it is one you are familiar with and have used before.**

1. *Multiple Choice* What is the exact value of $\cos \dfrac{5\pi}{12}$?

Ⓐ $\dfrac{\sqrt{2} + \sqrt{6}}{4}$ Ⓑ $\dfrac{\sqrt{2} - \sqrt{6}}{4}$

Ⓒ $\dfrac{\sqrt{3} - \sqrt{2}}{4}$ Ⓓ $\dfrac{\sqrt{3} + \sqrt{2}}{4}$

Ⓔ $\dfrac{\sqrt{6} - \sqrt{2}}{4}$

2. *Multiple Choice* What is the exact value of $\tan 330°$?

Ⓐ $\sqrt{3}$ Ⓑ $-\dfrac{\sqrt{3}}{3}$ Ⓒ $-\sqrt{3}$

Ⓓ $\dfrac{3}{\sqrt{3}}$ Ⓔ $-\dfrac{3}{\sqrt{3}}$

3. *Multiple Choice* If $\sin u = \dfrac{8}{17}$ with

$0 < u < \dfrac{\pi}{2}$ and $\cos v = -\dfrac{12}{13}$ with

$\pi < v < \dfrac{3\pi}{2}$, what is $\sin(u + v)$?

Ⓐ $\dfrac{56}{221}$ Ⓑ $-\dfrac{171}{221}$ Ⓒ $-\dfrac{56}{221}$

Ⓓ $\dfrac{8}{13}$ Ⓔ $-\dfrac{88}{221}$

4. *Multiple Choice* If $\cos u = \dfrac{4}{5}$ with

$\dfrac{3\pi}{2} < u < 2\pi$ and $\sin v = \dfrac{12}{13}$ with

$\dfrac{\pi}{2} < v < \pi$, what is $\cos(u - v)$?

Ⓐ $\dfrac{56}{65}$ Ⓑ $-\dfrac{16}{65}$ Ⓒ $\dfrac{16}{65}$

Ⓓ $-\dfrac{56}{65}$ Ⓔ $\dfrac{144}{65}$

5. *Multiple Choice* What is (are) the solution(s) of the equation

$$\cos\left(x - \dfrac{\pi}{4}\right) = \cos\left(x + \dfrac{\pi}{4}\right) - 1 \text{ in}$$

$0 \le x \le 2\pi$?

Ⓐ $\dfrac{5\pi}{4}, \dfrac{7\pi}{4}$ Ⓑ $\dfrac{3\pi}{4}, \dfrac{7\pi}{4}$ Ⓒ $\dfrac{\pi}{4}$

Ⓓ $\dfrac{\pi}{4}, \dfrac{7\pi}{4}$ Ⓔ $\dfrac{3\pi}{4}$

6. *Multiple Choice* What is (are) the solution(s) of the equation

$$\sin\left(x + \dfrac{\pi}{6}\right) + \sin\left(x - \dfrac{\pi}{6}\right) = 0 \text{ in}$$

$0 \le x \le \pi$?

Ⓐ $\dfrac{\pi}{3}, \dfrac{2\pi}{3}$ Ⓑ $\dfrac{\pi}{6}$ Ⓒ $0, \pi$

Ⓓ $0, \dfrac{\pi}{6}$ Ⓔ $\dfrac{\pi}{6}, \dfrac{\pi}{3}$

7. *Multi-Step Problem* A Ferris wheel with a radius 30 feet is rotating at a rate of 3 revolutions per minute. When $t = 0$, a chair starts at the lowest point on the wheel, which is 6 feet above the ground.

a. Write a model for the chair's height h (in feet) in the form of $h = a \cos bt + k$, where t is the time is seconds.

b. Graph the equation on a graphing calculator using a viewing window of $0 \le t \le 60$ and $-10 \le h \le 70$. What do you observe about the graph?

c. *Writing* Describe the chair's height h at each 10 second interval.

Standardized Test Practice

For use with pages 875–882

TEST TAKING STRATEGY   **When checking your answer to a question, try using a method different from one you used to get the answer.**

1. *Multiple Choice*   What is the exact value of tan 165°?

Ⓐ $\sqrt{3}$

Ⓑ $2 + \sqrt{3}$

Ⓒ $-2 + \sqrt{3}$

Ⓓ $\dfrac{-1 + \sqrt{3}}{2}$

Ⓔ $\dfrac{1 + \sqrt{3}}{2}$

2. *Multiple Choice*   What is the exact value of $\sin\dfrac{\pi}{12}$?

Ⓐ $\dfrac{\sqrt{2 - \sqrt{3}}}{2}$

Ⓑ $\dfrac{\sqrt{2} - \sqrt{3}}{2}$

Ⓒ $\dfrac{1}{2}$

Ⓓ $\dfrac{\sqrt{3}}{2}$

Ⓔ $\dfrac{\sqrt{3} - \sqrt{2}}{2}$

3. *Multiple Choice*   If $\cos u = -\dfrac{8}{17}$ with $\dfrac{\pi}{2} < u < \pi$, what does $\sin 2u$ equal?

Ⓐ $\dfrac{225}{289}$

Ⓑ $\dfrac{64}{289}$

Ⓒ $\dfrac{240}{289}$

Ⓓ $-\dfrac{240}{289}$

Ⓔ $-\dfrac{225}{289}$

4. *Multiple Choice*   If $\sin u = -\dfrac{4}{5}$ with $\pi < u < \dfrac{3\pi}{2}$, what does $\cos\dfrac{u}{2}$ equal?

Ⓐ $2\sqrt{10}$

Ⓑ $-\sqrt{10}$

Ⓒ $\dfrac{1}{\sqrt{10}}$

Ⓓ $-\dfrac{\sqrt{2}}{5}$

Ⓔ $-\dfrac{1}{\sqrt{5}}$

5. *Multiple Choice*   What is a solution of the equation $\tan\dfrac{x}{2} = \cos 2x$?

Ⓐ $\dfrac{3\pi}{2}$

Ⓑ $\dfrac{\pi}{2}$

Ⓒ $\dfrac{\pi}{4}$

Ⓓ $\dfrac{3\pi}{8}$

Ⓔ $\dfrac{7\pi}{4}$

Quantitative Comparison   **In Exercises 6–10, choose the statement below that is true about the given quantities.**

Ⓐ   The number in column A is greater.

Ⓑ   The number in column B is greater.

Ⓒ   The two numbers are equal.

Ⓓ   The relationship cannot be determined from the given information.

	Column A	Column B
6.	$\tan x$, with $45° < x < 90°$	$\tan\dfrac{x}{2}$, with $45° < x < 90°$
7.	$\cos x$, with $45° < x < 60°$	$\cos\dfrac{x}{2}$, with $45° < x < 60°$
8.	$\sin 2x$, with $90° < x < 180°$	$\sin\dfrac{x}{2}$, with $90° < x < 180°$
9.	$\cos 2x$, with $90° < x < 180°$	$\cos\dfrac{x}{2}$, with $90° < x < 180°$
10.	$\tan\dfrac{x}{2}$, with $45° < x < 60°$	$\cos 2x$, with $45° < x < 60°$

Chapter 14

Algebra 2
Standardized Test Practice Workbook

Cumulative Standardized Test Practice

For use after Chapter 14

1. *Multiple Choice* Which of the following is equivalent to $\log_6 216$?

    Ⓐ 36 Ⓑ $\frac{1}{6}$ Ⓒ 3

    Ⓓ 6 Ⓔ $\frac{1}{3}$

2. *Multiple Choice* What is the third term of the sequence defined by $a_n = -2n + 5$?

    Ⓐ 3 Ⓑ 1 Ⓒ 5

    Ⓓ -3 Ⓔ -1

3. *Multiple Choice* To win a state lottery, a player must correctly match six different numbers from 1 to 49. If a computer randomly assigns six numbers per ticket, how many tickets would a person have to buy to have a 1% chance of winning?

    Ⓐ at least 14,054

    Ⓑ at least 1405

    Ⓒ at least 140,542

    Ⓓ at least 140

    Ⓔ at least 1,405,420

4. *Multiple Choice* Which of the following is equivalent to 330°?

    Ⓐ $\frac{5\pi}{6}$ Ⓑ $\frac{11\pi}{6}$ Ⓒ $\frac{7\pi}{3}$

    Ⓓ $\frac{7\pi}{6}$ Ⓔ $\frac{11\pi}{3}$

Quantitative Comparison **In Exercises 5–11, choose the statement that is true about the given quantities.**

   Ⓐ The number in column A is greater.

   Ⓑ The number in column B is greater.

   Ⓒ The two numbers are equal.

   Ⓓ The relationship cannot be determined from the given information.

	Column A	Column B
5.	$\sum_{n=1}^{4} (n^2 + 1)$	$\sum_{n=1}^{4} (2n + 5)$
6.	The number of permutations of 18 objects taken 3 at a time	The number of permutations of 9 objects taken 6 at a time
7.	The area of a sector with $r = 5$ cm and $\theta = 60°$	The area of a sector with $r = 2.5$ cm and $\theta = 90°$
8.	Amplitude of the graph of $y = -6 \cos 4x$	Amplitude of the graph of $y = 6 \sin 7x$
9.	$f(2)$ where $f(x) = \log_4 x$	$\frac{1}{2}$
10.	The solution of $\frac{x}{5} + \frac{1}{2} = \frac{x-2}{3}$	The solution of $\frac{x}{4} - \frac{1}{5} = \frac{2x-1}{2}$
11.	$\cos \frac{7\pi}{12}$	$\sin \frac{5\pi}{12}$

12. *Multiple Choice* What is the product $\frac{x^2 - 2x - 24}{x^2 - 9x + 18} \cdot \frac{x^2 + x - 12}{x^2 - 16}$?

    Ⓐ $x - 4$ Ⓑ $\frac{1}{x - 4}$

    Ⓒ $x + 4$ Ⓓ $\frac{1}{x + 4}$

    Ⓔ $\frac{x + 4}{x - 4}$

13. *Multiple Choice* What is the vertex of the graph of $y = \frac{1}{2}(x - 4)^2 + 5$?

Ⓐ $(0, 5)$ Ⓑ $(4, -5)$

Ⓒ $(-4, 37)$ Ⓓ $(4, 5)$ Ⓔ $(2, 7)$

14. *Multiple Choice* What is the solution of $\log_4(2x - 7) = \log_4(3x - 13)$?

Ⓐ -2 Ⓑ 0 Ⓒ 6
Ⓓ 2 Ⓔ -6

15. *Multiple Choice* Which equation represents the perpendicular bisector of the line segment connecting the points $(-4, 6)$ and $(2, 8)$?

Ⓐ $y = 3x - 4$ Ⓑ $y = -3x + 4$
Ⓒ $y = x + 4$ Ⓓ $y = 3x + 4$
Ⓔ $y = -3x - 4$

16. *Multiple Choice* Which function is the inverse of $f(x) = -2x - 11$?

Ⓐ $f^{-1}(x) = \frac{1}{2}x - 11$

Ⓑ $f^{-1}(x) = -2x + 11$

Ⓒ $f^{-1}(x) = -\frac{1}{2}x - \frac{11}{2}$

Ⓓ $f^{-1}(x) = -\frac{1}{2}x + \frac{11}{2}$

Ⓔ $f^{-1}(x) = 2x + 11$

17. *Multiple Choice* If $\sin \theta = -\frac{4}{5}$ and $\pi < \theta < \frac{3\pi}{2}$, which of the following is true?

Ⓐ $\cos \theta = -\frac{5}{3}$ Ⓑ $\tan \theta = \frac{3}{4}$

Ⓒ $\tan \theta = -\frac{4}{3}$ Ⓓ $\sec \theta = -\frac{5}{3}$

Ⓔ $\cos \theta = \frac{3}{5}$

18. *Multiple Choice* What is the sum of the first 15 terms of the series

$2 + 11 + 20 + 29 + \ldots$?

Ⓐ 975 Ⓑ 1015 Ⓒ 1145
Ⓓ 1165 Ⓔ 1275

19. *Multi-Step Problem* Two motorized toy boats are released in a pool at time $t = 0$. Boat 1 travels 35° north of east at a rate of 0.65 meter per second. Boat 2 travels due east at a rate of 0.4 meter per second.

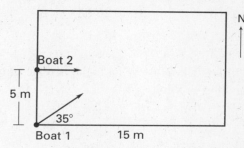

a. Write a set of parametric equations to describe the path of each boat.

b. At what point will each boat hit the east edge of the pool?

c. At what point do the paths of the two boats cross?

d. *Writing* If the two boats are released at the same time, will they collide? If so, how many seconds after the boats are released? If not, explain why not.

20. *Multiple Choice* Which of the following is a factor of the polynomial $3x^3 - 7x^2 - 22x + 8$?

Ⓐ $(3x - 1)$ Ⓑ $(x + 1)$
Ⓒ $(3x - 2)$ Ⓓ $(3x + 1)$
Ⓔ $(2x - 1)$

21. *Multiple Choice*   How many different license plates are possible if 4 digits are followed by two letters?

Ⓐ 67,600   Ⓑ 676,000

Ⓒ 67,000   Ⓓ 6,760,000

Ⓔ 670,600

22. *Multiple Choice*   What is the approximate horizontal distance traveled by a football that is kicked at an angle of 50° with an initial speed of 65 feet per second?

Ⓐ 103 ft   Ⓑ 126 ft   Ⓒ 130 ft

Ⓓ 145 ft   Ⓔ 152 ft

23. *Multiple Choice*   What is the inverse of the function $y = \log_7 x$?

Ⓐ $y = 7^x$ Ⓑ $y = 7x$

Ⓒ $y = \dfrac{1}{7}x$ Ⓓ $y = x^7$

Ⓔ $y = \dfrac{1}{7^x}$

24. *Multiple Choice*   Which function is graphed?

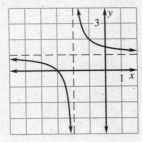

Ⓐ

$f(x) = \dfrac{1}{x-2} - 1$

Ⓑ $f(x) = \dfrac{1}{x+2} - 1$

Ⓒ $f(x) = \dfrac{1}{x-2} + 1$

Ⓓ $f(x) = \dfrac{1}{x+2} + 1$

Ⓔ None of these

25. *Multiple Choice*   Given the triangle where $A = 28°$ and $a = 8$ cm, what is the approximate value of b?

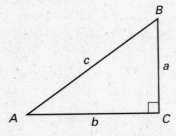

Ⓐ 0.066 cm   Ⓑ 15.0 cm

Ⓒ 7.06 cm   Ⓓ 17.0 cm

Ⓔ 9.06 cm

26. *Multiple Choice*   Which of the following is the factorization of $x^3 - 18x^2 + 96x - 128$?

Ⓐ $(x - 2)(x + 2)(x + 8)$

Ⓑ $(x - 8)^2(x + 2)$

Ⓒ $(x - 2)(x + 8)^2$

Ⓓ $(x - 8)(x + 8)(x - 2)$

Ⓔ $(x - 8)^2(x - 2)$

27. *Multiple Choice*   What is the focus of the parabola with equation $64y = x^2$?

Ⓐ (64, 0)   Ⓑ (16, 0)

Ⓒ (0, 16)   Ⓓ (0, −64)

Ⓔ (0, 64)

28. *Multiple Choice*   A dart thrown at the square target shown is equally likely to hit anywhere inside the target. What is the probability that the dart hits the shaded region?

Ⓐ $\dfrac{6}{9}$ Ⓑ $\dfrac{9}{36}$ Ⓒ $\dfrac{6}{81}$

Ⓓ $\dfrac{36}{9}$ Ⓔ $\dfrac{36}{81}$

Cumulative Standardized Test Practice

For use after Chapter 14

Quantitative Comparison **In Exercises 29–33, choose the statement that is true about the given quantities.**

Ⓐ The number in column A is greater.

Ⓑ The number in column B is greater.

Ⓒ The two numbers are equal.

Ⓓ The relationship cannot be determined from the given information.

	Column A	Column B
29.	$3 - 15 \div 5 + 6 \cdot 4$	$12 \div 2 + 3(11 - 5)$
30.	k where z varies jointly with x and y; $z = 100$ and $y = 10$ when $x = 5$	k where z varies inversely with x and directly with y; $z = 12$ and $y = 2$ when $x = 3$
31.	$_6C_3$	$_8C_4$
32.	Distance between $(5, 8)$ and $(1, -4)$	Distance between $(2, 9)$ and $(-1, -6)$
33.	The value of $\sec 310°$	The value of $\tan 150°$

34. *Multiple Choice* What is the approximate area of a triangle with $A = 31°$, $b = 10$, and $c = 18$?

Ⓐ 108.2   Ⓑ 54.1   Ⓒ 158.5

Ⓓ 46.4   Ⓔ 92.7

35. *Multiple Choice* Suppose you deposit $15,600 in an account that pays 6.5% annual interest. What is the balance after two years if the interest is compounded monthly?

Ⓐ $15,769.46   Ⓑ $16,644.76

Ⓒ $17,354.27   Ⓓ $17,585.04

Ⓔ $17,759.49

36. *Multiple Choice* What is the factorization of $f(x) = 2x^3 - 7x^2 - 53x + 28$ given that $f(-4) = 0$?

Ⓐ $(x - 4)(2x + 1)(x + 7)$

Ⓑ $(x - 7)(2x - 1)(x + 4)$

Ⓒ $(x - 4)(2x + 1)(x - 7)$

Ⓓ $(x - 7)(2x - 1)(x - 4)$

Ⓔ $(x + 4)(2x + 1)(x - 7)$

37. *Multiple Choice* Which is the standard form of the equation where the point $(-5, 8)$ is on a circle whose center is the origin?

Ⓐ $x^2 - y^2 = 40$ Ⓑ $x^2 + y^2 = 89$

Ⓒ $x^2 + y^2 = 40$ Ⓓ $x^2 - y^2 = 8$

Ⓔ $x^2 + y^2 = 8$

38. *Multiple Choice* If $P(A) = 0.57$, $P(B) = 0.16$, and $P(A \text{ and } B) = 0.11$, what is $P(A \text{ or } B)$?

Ⓐ 0.14   Ⓑ 0.26   Ⓒ 0.32

Ⓓ 0.38   Ⓔ 0.62

39. *Multiple Choice* What fraction is equivalent to the repeating decimal 8.18181. . . ?

Ⓐ $\dfrac{58}{7}$ Ⓑ $\dfrac{107}{13}$ Ⓒ $\dfrac{90}{11}$

Ⓓ $\dfrac{154}{19}$ Ⓔ $\dfrac{220}{27}$

40. *Multiple Choice* What is the period of the graph of $y = \dfrac{2}{3}\sin 5x$?

Ⓐ 5π Ⓑ $\dfrac{5\pi}{2}$ Ⓒ $\dfrac{3\pi}{4}$

Ⓓ $\dfrac{2\pi}{5}$ Ⓔ $\dfrac{2}{3}$

Test-Taking Tips for Students

For use before the End-of-Course Test

Test-Taking Strategies

To do a task well, you need both competence and confidence. A person playing the guitar for the first time will not sound like a professional, but even a talented guitarist may perform poorly if he or she is tense and worried.

To perform well on a test, you must have the necessary knowledge and problem-solving skills—you must be *competent* in the subject matter. The most important part of test preparation comes from your everyday work during the school year. If you keep up with your homework, pay attention and ask questions in class, and work to understand each new topic as it comes up, you will develop the knowledge you need to perform well on tests. However, there are strategies that will help you apply your knowledge efficiently and avoid obstacles.

You also need to feel *confident* in your test-taking abilities. While success itself is the best confidence booster, there are some simple things you can do that will help you go into a test feeling relaxed and self-assured.

Before the Test

It is difficult to do well on a test when you are tired, hungry, and nervous. The following strategies will help you be at your best when the test begins.

Take one or more practice tests. Taking a practice test is like rehearsing for a play or going to basketball practice. Practice tests help you understand what the real thing will be like and help you identify areas you may need work on.

Get a full night's sleep. Don't stay up too late the night before an important test, even if you are trying to do last-minute "cramming." A good night's sleep will help you concentrate during the test.

Eat a good breakfast. You need a healthy breakfast to be alert and resourceful during a test, especially a long one.

Be on time, and be prepared. It's hard to do your best on a test when you arrive 5 minutes late and without a pencil. (It's also difficult for your classmates to concentrate while you look for an empty desk!) Being on time will give you a few moments to relax before the test begins.

Choose a good seat. Will you be distracted if you sit near a corner or by your friends? Is there a noisy heater along one wall? Select a comfortable place away from distractions.

Be positive. Try not to be intimidated by a test, even one that is especially important. Go into the room ready to show off how much you know.

During the Test

To do your best on a test, you need to work steadily and efficiently. The following ideas will help you keep on track.

Read questions carefully. Before you begin to answer a question, read it completely. Key information may come at the end of the question. Reread the question if you are not sure you understand what it is asking.

Don't read the answers too soon. Whenever possible, answer the question before looking at the answer choices. Even if you cannot come up with the answer right away, your first try may help you understand the question better and eliminate some answers.

Read all choices before marking your answer. Be sure you know all of your options before choosing an answer. If you are having difficulty understanding a question, the answer choices may help you understand what that question is asking.

Pace yourself. Don't try to go through the test as quickly as you can—this can lead to careless mistakes. Work steadily.

Don't get distracted. Resist the temptation to look up every time you hear a rustling paper or a scooting desk. Focus on *your* paper and *your* thought process.

Don't look for patterns. Especially on standardized tests, there is *no way* to tell what answer comes next by looking at previous answers. Don't waste precious time looking for a pattern that isn't there.

Mark your answer sheet carefully. Take a moment to make sure you mark your answer

Test-Taking Tips for Students (continued)

in the correct place. This is especially important if you skip one or more problems. When answering multiple-choice tests, be sure to fill in the bubble completely and, if you change an answer, to erase all traces of your old mark.

Check your answers. If you have time, go back and check your answers, filling in answers to any problems you may have skipped. *However . . .*

Be SURE before you change an answer. Your first answer is usually your best answer. Don't change an answer unless you are certain the original answer is incorrect.

If you get stuck, it is important to stay relaxed and confident even if you struggle with some problems. (Even the best test-takers are stumped occasionally!) The following tips will help you work through any temporary setbacks.

Stay calm. Realize that this is only a small part of the test. Don't let a momentary obstacle affect your confidence.

Don't spend too much time on one problem. If you find a problem especially difficult, move on to others that are easier for you. Make the best guess you can and go on, or skip the problem entirely and return to it later if time permits.

Make an educated guess. If you know some of the answer choices are wrong, eliminate those and make the best guess you can from the rest.

> **Example** Find the quotient $-56 \div (-8)$.
>
> A -8 B -7
>
> C 7 D 8

There are two parts to this answer, the positive-or-negative sign and the actual number. Since you know the quotient of two negative numbers must *always* be positive, you can eliminate answer choices **A** and **B**.

You may remember $8 \times 8 = 64$, so $7 \times 8 = 56$. Therefore $56 \div 8 = 7$. The correct answer is **C**.

Work backward. If you are having a difficult time with a problem, you may be able to substitute the answers into the problem and see which one is correct.

Which equation is a function rule for the input-output table shown?

> **Example** Which equation is a function rule for the input-output table shown?
>
> | x | 0 | 2 | 4 | 6 | 8 |
> |-----|---|---|---|---|----|
> | y | 2 | 4 | 6 | 8 | 10 |
>
> A $y = \frac{x}{2}$ B $y = 2x$
>
> C $y = x - 2$ D $y = x + 2$

To test possible answer choices, use the easiest values from the input-output table. From the table, you know that if $x = 0$ then $y = 2$.

In choice **A**, substitute 0 for x and you find that $y = 0$. So **A** is not correct.

To test choice **B**, again substitute 0 for x and you find that once more $y = 0$. So **B** is not correct.

When you test choice **C** in the same manner, you find that $y = -2$, so **C** is not correct.

In answer choice **D**, when you substitute 0 in place of x, you find that $y = 2$. **D** is the correct answer.

On open-ended problems, be sure your answer covers all that is being asked. Show all of your work and explain your steps or reasoning. Include a diagram if necessary. After you finish your answer, go back and reread the question to make sure you have not left anything out.

After the Test

Reward yourself. If possible, take some time to relax after the test.

Make a plan for the next test. Review what you did before and during the test. Decide which techniques and strategies worked well for you and which ones were not helpful. Think about what you will do differently next time.

Learn from the test. Find out what types of problems caused you the most difficulty and what types you did well on. This will help you prepare for future tests.

Build your confidence for next time. Even if the test did not go well, there are probably some areas where you did succeed. Congratulate yourself on what you did well, and resolve to learn from your mistakes.

Name _____   Date _____

End-of-Course Test Answer Sheet

1. Ⓐ Ⓑ Ⓒ Ⓓ
2. Ⓕ Ⓖ Ⓗ Ⓙ
3. Ⓐ Ⓑ Ⓒ Ⓓ
4. Ⓕ Ⓖ Ⓗ Ⓙ
5. Ⓐ Ⓑ Ⓒ Ⓓ
6. Ⓕ Ⓖ Ⓗ Ⓙ
7. Ⓐ Ⓑ Ⓒ Ⓓ
8. Ⓕ Ⓖ Ⓗ Ⓙ
9. Ⓐ Ⓑ Ⓒ Ⓓ
10. Ⓕ Ⓖ Ⓗ Ⓙ
11. Ⓐ Ⓑ Ⓒ Ⓓ
12. Ⓕ Ⓖ Ⓗ Ⓙ
13. Ⓐ Ⓑ Ⓒ Ⓓ
14. Ⓕ Ⓖ Ⓗ Ⓙ
15. Ⓐ Ⓑ Ⓒ Ⓓ
16. Ⓕ Ⓖ Ⓗ Ⓙ
17. Ⓐ Ⓑ Ⓒ Ⓓ

18. Ⓕ Ⓖ Ⓗ Ⓙ
19. Ⓐ Ⓑ Ⓒ Ⓓ
20. Ⓕ Ⓖ Ⓗ Ⓙ
21. Ⓐ Ⓑ Ⓒ Ⓓ
22. Ⓕ Ⓖ Ⓗ Ⓙ
23. Ⓐ Ⓑ Ⓒ Ⓓ
24. Ⓕ Ⓖ Ⓗ Ⓙ
25. Ⓐ Ⓑ Ⓒ Ⓓ
26. Ⓕ Ⓖ Ⓗ Ⓙ
27. Ⓐ Ⓑ Ⓒ Ⓓ
28. Ⓕ Ⓖ Ⓗ Ⓙ
29. Ⓐ Ⓑ Ⓒ Ⓓ
30. Ⓕ Ⓖ Ⓗ Ⓙ
31. Ⓐ Ⓑ Ⓒ Ⓓ
32. Ⓕ Ⓖ Ⓗ Ⓙ
33. Ⓐ Ⓑ Ⓒ Ⓓ
34. Ⓕ Ⓖ Ⓗ Ⓙ

35. Ⓐ Ⓑ Ⓒ Ⓓ
36. Ⓕ Ⓖ Ⓗ Ⓙ
37. Ⓐ Ⓑ Ⓒ Ⓓ
38. Ⓕ Ⓖ Ⓗ Ⓙ
39. Ⓐ Ⓑ Ⓒ Ⓓ
40. Ⓕ Ⓖ Ⓗ Ⓙ
41. Ⓐ Ⓑ Ⓒ Ⓓ
42. Ⓕ Ⓖ Ⓗ Ⓙ
43. Ⓐ Ⓑ Ⓒ Ⓓ
44. Ⓕ Ⓖ Ⓗ Ⓙ
45. Ⓐ Ⓑ Ⓒ Ⓓ
46. Ⓕ Ⓖ Ⓗ Ⓙ
47. Ⓐ Ⓑ Ⓒ Ⓓ
48. Ⓕ Ⓖ Ⓗ Ⓙ
49. Ⓐ Ⓑ Ⓒ Ⓓ
50. Ⓕ Ⓖ Ⓗ Ⓙ

Algebra 2
Standardized Test Practice Workbook

End-of-Course Test

DIRECTIONS
Read and solve each question. For this test you may assume that the value of the denominator of a rational expression is not zero.

1 Which of the following equations shows an example of the Commutative Property of Multiplication?

- **A** $3z^2 \times (2z \times 4) = (3z^2 \times 2z) \times 4$
- **B** $3z^2 \times \frac{1}{3z^2} = 1$
- **C** $3z^2 \times (2z \times 4) = 3z^2 \times (4 \times 2z)$
- **D** $3z^2 \times 1 = 3z^2$

2 Which of the following is *not* a true statement?

- **F** Matrix addition is commutative.
- **G** Matrix addition is associative.
- **H** Matrix multiplication is commutative.
- **J** Scalar multiplication is associative.

3 Which expression is equal to $\frac{3}{2r} + \frac{2}{3}$?

- **A** $\frac{5}{2r + 3}$
- **B** $\frac{5}{6r}$
- **C** $\frac{6r + 6}{6r}$
- **D** $\frac{9 + 4r}{6r}$

4 Which expression is equivalent to $\dfrac{\frac{x}{x^2 - 1}}{\frac{x + 1}{x - 1}}$?

- **F** $\frac{x}{(x + 1)^2}$
- **G** $\frac{x}{(x - 1)^2}$
- **H** $\frac{1}{x + 1}$
- **J** $\frac{1}{x}$

5 Which is equivalent to $\sqrt[4]{\frac{16a^2}{81b^4}}$?

- **A** $\frac{4a}{9b^2}$
- **B** $\frac{4a^{\frac{1}{2}}}{3b}$
- **C** $\frac{2a^2}{3b^2}$
- **D** $\frac{2a^{\frac{1}{2}}}{3b}$

6 Which is equivalent to $\sqrt{x^5}$?

- **F** $x^{\frac{2}{5}}$
- **G** $x^{\frac{5}{2}}$
- **H** x^{10}
- **J** $x^{\frac{1}{10}}$

7 Which is a factor of $x^2 + 5x - 6$?

- **A** $x - 3$
- **B** $x - 2$
- **C** $x + 5$
- **D** $x + 6$

8 What is the factorization of $x^4 - 64$?

    F $(x^2 + 8)^2$

    G $(x^2 - 8)^2$

    H $(x^2 - 8)(x^2 + 8)$

    J $x^2(x^2 - 64)$

9 Which is equivalent to i^6?

    A i

    B 1

    C $^-1$

    D ^-i

10 Which is equivalent to $(5 - 4i)^2$?

    F 9

    G 41

    H $41 - 40i$

    J $9 - 40i$

11 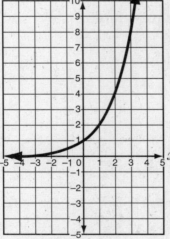 Which is most likely the equation of the graph to the left?

    A $y = 2^x$

    B $y = 2 + x$

    C $y = x^2$

    D $y = \sqrt{x}$

12 Which is most likely the graph of $y = {}^-x^2 + 3$?

    F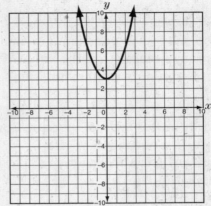

    G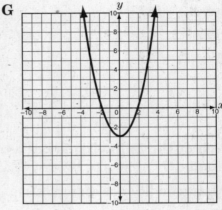

    H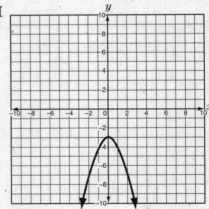

    J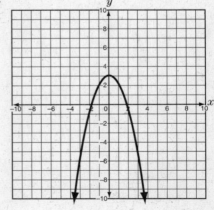

13 What is the domain of the function $f(x) = \sqrt{x - 9}$?

    A $x \geq 9$

    B $x \geq 0$

    C $y \geq 0$

    D $y \geq 3$

14 For what value of y does the ordered pair $(3, y)$ lie on the graph of $f(x) = 2x^3 - 4x + 1$?

    F 3

    G 7

    H 43

    J 67

15 Which is a zero of the function $f(x) = 2x^3 - 6x - 4$?

    A $^-2$

    B 0

    C 1

    D 2

16 Which is most likely the graph of a logarithmic function?

F

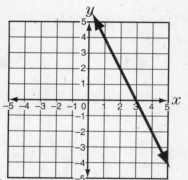

G

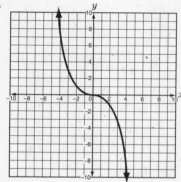

H

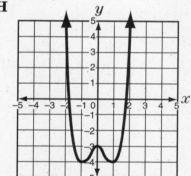

J

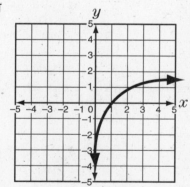

17

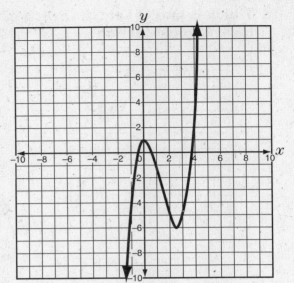

Which type of function is shown in the graph?

A Cubic

B Exponential

C Linear

D Absolute value

18 If $a_n = 4 + 2^{n-1}$, what is the value of a_4?

F 4

G 12

H 20

J 216

19 Which is equivalent to $\sum\limits_{n=1}^{4} 3n$?

A 30

B 12

C 10

D 6

20 Which equation best describes the data shown in the scatterplot?

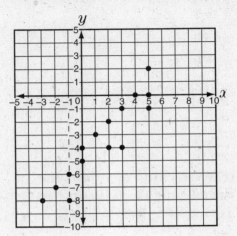

F $y = 5 - x$

G $y = x - 5$

H $y = 5x - 1$

J $y = {}^-x - 5$

21 Which type of function best describes the data in the scatterplot below?

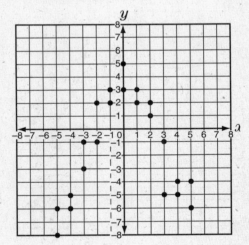

A Linear

B Quadratic

C Logarithmic

D Exponential

22 The relationship between the amount of a fine for a speeding ticket and the number of miles over the speed limit is linear.

Excess speed (mi/h)	Fine ($)
5	$70
12	$84
18	$96
25	$110

What fine would be given for an excess speed of 36 mi/h?

F $252

G $192

H $132

J $120

23

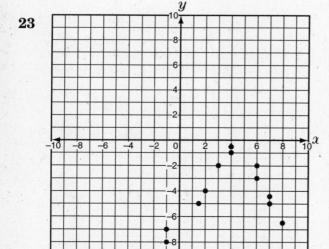

Which equation most closely fits the data in this scatterplot?

A $\frac{1}{4}y = x^2 + 4$

B $y = -\frac{1}{2}(x - 4)^2$

C $y = x^2 - 16$

D $2y = (x + 4)^2$

24 The chart gives the number of new textbooks ordered in a school district.

Year	Number of Books
2000	505
2001	248
2002	126
2003	65

Assuming an exponential relationship, which is the best estimate for the number of new textbooks ordered in 2004?

F 10

G 25

H 32

J 44

25 The time it takes a truck driver to travel a given distance varies inversely as his average speed. If it takes 3.5 hours to travel 217 miles, how long will it take him to travel 310 miles?

A 4 hours 45 minutes

B 5 hours

C 5 hours 30 minutes

D 6 hours

26 If y varies jointly as a and b^2, and k is the constant of variation, which equation shows the relationship among y, a, and b?

F $y = k\dfrac{a}{b^2}$

G $y = kab^2$

H $y = \dfrac{ab^2}{k}$

J $y = \dfrac{k}{ab^2}$

27 Which is the solution set for $|2x + 1| = 5$?

A $\{^-5\}$

B $\{^-3\}$

C $\{2, ^-3\}$

D $\{3, ^-3\}$

28 Which shows the solution set for $|x + 4| < 2$?

F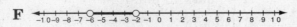

G

H

J

29 What are the solutions to $5x^2 - 6x + 3 = 0$?

A $\dfrac{3 \pm 2\sqrt{6}}{5}$

B $\dfrac{3 \pm 2i\sqrt{6}}{5}$

C $\dfrac{3 \pm i\sqrt{6}}{5}$

D $\dfrac{3 \pm 4\sqrt{6}}{5}$

30 Which of the following quadratic equations can not be solved by factoring?

F $x^2 + 5x - 6 = 0$

G $x^2 - x + 6 = 0$

H $x^2 + x - 6 = 0$

J $x^2 - 5x - 6 = 0$

31 The graphs of $f(x) = \sqrt{2x + 1}$ and $g(x) = 3\sqrt{x} - 3$ are shown below.

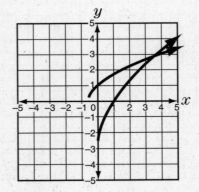

What is the solution to $\sqrt{2x + 1} = 3\sqrt{x} - 3$?

A 4

B 3

C $-\dfrac{1}{2}$

D $^-3$

32 For which value of x does
$$\frac{3x+1}{4} = \frac{2x+5}{8}?$$

F 6

G $\frac{3}{8}$

H $\frac{3}{4}$

J $\frac{7}{4}$

33 Which inequality has no solution?

A $|3x - 9| > {}^-5$

B $|3x - 9| < {}^-5$

C $|3x| - 9 < 5$

D $3|x - 3| > 5$

34 On which graph does the shaded area show the solution set of the equation $y \le \left|\frac{1}{2}x - 3\right|$?

F
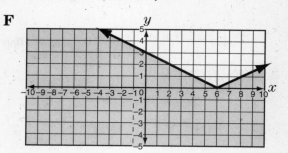

G
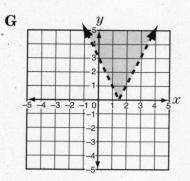

H
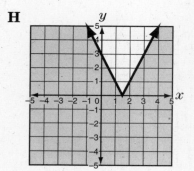

J
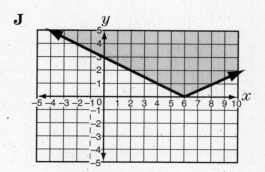

35 What is the solution set for
$2x^2 - 7x - 3 = 0$?

A $\left\{\frac{1}{2}, 3\right\}$

B $\left\{\frac{49 \pm \sqrt{31}}{2}\right\}$

C $\left\{\frac{1}{2}, {}^-3\right\}$

D $\left\{\frac{7 \pm \sqrt{73}}{4}\right\}$

36 What is the solution for
$\sqrt[3]{3 + 2x} = 2\sqrt[3]{x}$?

F 0

G $\frac{1}{2}$

H 2

J 3

37

What are the factors of the
polynomial function shown?

A $(x - 1)$, $(x + 2)$, and $(x + 4)$

B $(x + 1)$, $(x - 2)$, and $(x - 4)$

C $(x - 1)$, $(x - 2)$, and $(x + 4)$

D $(x + 1)$, $(x + 2)$, and $(x - 4)$

38 For what value(s) of a does the
graph of $f(x) = 2x^2 - 7x - 4$ contain
the point $(a, 0)$?

F $^-4$

G $-\frac{1}{2}$, 4

H 1, $^-2$

J $-\frac{1}{2}$

39 Which figure is described by the
equation $\frac{(x - 2)^2}{25} + \frac{(y - 4)^2}{9} = 1$?

A Circle

B Ellipse

C Hyperbola

D Parabola

40 Which of these is the equation of
a hyperbola?

F $4(x + 3)^2 + (y + 2)^2 = 16$

G $\frac{(x - 1)^2}{4} + \frac{y}{9} = 1$

H $9(x + 4)^2 - 4(y - 2)^2 = 36$

J $\frac{(x - 6)^2}{81} + \frac{(y - 2)^2}{81} = 1$

41 What are the zeroes of the function
$f(x) = 2x(x - 3)(x + 5)$?

A 2, 3, and 5

B $^-3$ and $^-5$

C 3 and 5

D 0, 3, and $^-5$

42 Which of the following is the graph of $\dfrac{(x-5)^2}{16} + \dfrac{(x+3)^2}{16} = 1$?

F

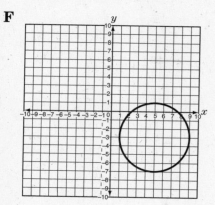

G

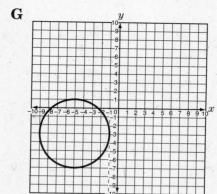

H

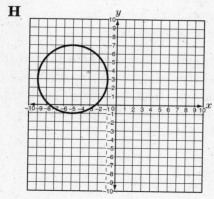

J

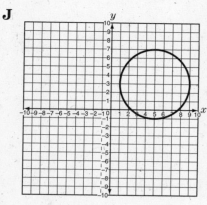

43 A convenience store sells three flavors of iced drinks in three different sizes. Matrix X shows the number of each flavor sold one day.

	Size		
Flavor	**S**	**M**	**L**
Citrus	25	31	46
Cola	48	12	8
Cherry	19	28	41

$= X$

Matrix Y shows the cost of each size.

	Cost
S	$0.79
M	$1.19
L	$1.49

$= Y$

Which matrix shows the total amount of the sales of each flavor?

A

Citrus	$72.68
Cola	$84.49
Cherry	$141.55

B

Citrus	$125.18
Cola	$64.12
Cherry	$109.42

C

Citrus	$80.58
Cola	$80.92
Cherry	$131.12

D

Citrus	$88.01
Cola	$76.32
Cherry	$115.09

44

$$A = \begin{bmatrix} 2 & 1 & ^-2 \\ 3 & ^-1 & 0 \\ 2 & 0 & 5 \end{bmatrix} \quad B = \begin{bmatrix} 1 & 2 & 0 \\ 3 & 1 & ^-2 \\ 4 & ^-3 & 1 \end{bmatrix}$$

Which matrix shows the product
$B \times A$?

F $\begin{bmatrix} 2 & 2 & 0 \\ 9 & ^-1 & 0 \\ 8 & 0 & 5 \end{bmatrix}$

G $\begin{bmatrix} 3 & 3 & ^-2 \\ 6 & 0 & ^-2 \\ 6 & ^-3 & 6 \end{bmatrix}$

H $\begin{bmatrix} 8 & ^-1 & ^-2 \\ 5 & 2 & ^-16 \\ 1 & 7 & ^-3 \end{bmatrix}$

J $\begin{bmatrix} ^-3 & 11 & ^-4 \\ 0 & 5 & 2 \\ 22 & ^-11 & 5 \end{bmatrix}$

45 Which matrix equation represents this system of linear equations?

$$\begin{cases} 3x - y = 13 \\ x + 2y = 2 \end{cases}$$

A $\begin{bmatrix} 3 & ^-1 \\ 1 & 2 \end{bmatrix}\begin{bmatrix} x \\ y \end{bmatrix} = \begin{bmatrix} 13 \\ 2 \end{bmatrix}$

B $\begin{bmatrix} x & y \end{bmatrix} = \begin{bmatrix} 3 & ^-1 \\ 1 & 2 \end{bmatrix}\begin{bmatrix} 13 & 2 \end{bmatrix}$

C $\begin{bmatrix} x \\ y \end{bmatrix} = \begin{bmatrix} 3 & ^-1 \\ 1 & 2 \end{bmatrix}\begin{bmatrix} 13 \\ 2 \end{bmatrix}$

D $\begin{bmatrix} 3 & ^-1 & 13 \\ 1 & 2 & 2 \end{bmatrix} = \begin{bmatrix} x \\ y \end{bmatrix}$

46 Bonita has pennies, dimes, and nickels worth \$0.88 in her purse. The number of pennies is twice the number of nickels, and the number of dimes is two less than the number of pennies.

Which system of equations can be solved to determine the number of pennies p, the number of nickels n, and the number of dimes d, in Bonita's purse?

F $p + n + d = 0.88$
$p = 2n$
$d = 2 - p$

G $0.01p + 0.05n + 0.10d = 0.88$
$p = 2n$
$d = 2 - p$

H $p + n + d = 88$
$p = 2n$
$d = p - 2$

G $0.01p + 0.05n + 0.10d = 0.88$
$p = 2n$
$d = p - 2$

47

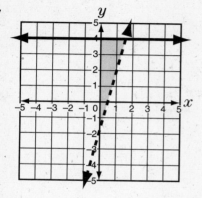

Which system of inequalities is represented by the graph shown above?

A $\begin{cases} y < 4 \\ x > 0 \\ y \le 4x - 2 \end{cases}$

B $\begin{cases} y \le 4 \\ x \ge 0 \\ y < 4x - 2 \end{cases}$

C $\begin{cases} y \le 4 \\ x \ge 0 \\ y > 4x - 2 \end{cases}$

D $\begin{cases} y < 4 \\ x > 0 \\ y \ge 4x - 2 \end{cases}$

48 The graph below shows the daily sales goal for the manager of a small flower shop.

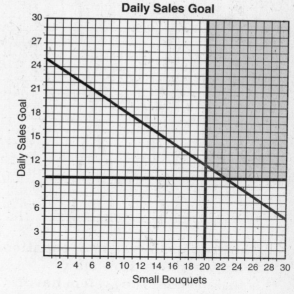

Which of the following statements about the sales goal is true?

F The minimum number of large bouquets that must be sold is 25.

G The goal is met if 30 small bouquets and 5 large bouquets are sold.

H The minimum number of small bouquets that must be sold is 10.

J The goal is met if 20 small bouquets and 12 large bouquets are sold.

49 What are the real-number solutions to the following system of equations?

$$\begin{cases} y^2 = 5x + 12 \\ x^2 + y^2 = 36 \end{cases}$$

A $\{(3, 27), (3, ^-27)\}$

B $\{(3, 3\sqrt{3}), (3, ^-3\sqrt{3})\}$

C $\{(^-8, 28), (^-8, ^-28)\}$

D $\{(^-8, 2\sqrt{7}), (^-8, ^-2\sqrt{7})\}$

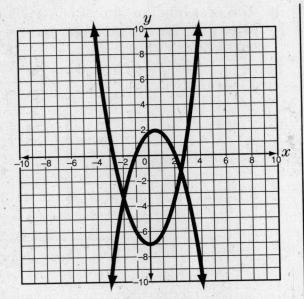

The graph of a system of equations is shown above. How many solutions does the system have?

F 1

G 2

H 3

J 4